ABOUT THE AUTHOR

Michael Rosen is renowned for his work as a poet, performer, broadcaster and scriptwriter. He visits schools with his one-man show to enthuse children with his passion for books and poetry. In 2007 he was appointed Children's Laureate, a role which he held until 2009. While Laureate, he set up The Roald Dahl Funny Prize. He currently lives in London with his wife and children. *Many Different Kinds of Love*, his account of his experience of coronavirus, was published in 2021 and was an instant *Sunday Times* bestseller.

PRAISE FOR *GETTING BETTER*

'If I could prescribe *Getting Better* to the entire nation, I would. It's so gloriously full of the warmth, wisdom and incredible honesty that mean Michael is loved by adults and children alike. It's a book that inspires hope, courage and belief in humanity. Basically, it reminds you how to live. I loved every single word'
Dr Rachel Clarke

'In some ways, this is a quirky and intimate memoir. But Rosen has become that curious thing, a national treasure, and this book perhaps reflects the national mood – and the national need, even – better than a grander account of Covid might' *The Times*

'Like having a cup of tea and a chat with Michael himself. Just full to the brim with wisdom, truth and beautiful silliness' *Cariad Lloyd*

'Funny and very moving' *Daily Mail*

'A survivor's manual' *Guardian*

GETTING BETTER

BETTER

Life lessons on going under, getting over it, and getting through it

MICHAEL ROSEN

5

Ebury Press, an imprint of Ebury Publishing
20 Vauxhall Bridge Road
London SW1V 2SA

Ebury Press is part of the Penguin Random House group of companies
whose addresses can be found at global.penguinrandomhouse.com

First published by Ebury Press in 2023
This edition published by Ebury Press in 2024

www.penguin.co.uk

A CIP catalogue record for this book is available from the British Library

ISBN 9781529148909

Typeset in 12.24/16.6pt Baskerville MT Pro by Jouve (UK), Milton Keynes
Printed and bound in Great Britain by Clays Ltd, Elcograf S.p.A.

The authorised representative in the EEA is Penguin Random House Ireland,
Morrison Chambers, 32 Nassau Street, Dublin D02 YH68

Penguin Random House is committed to a sustainable future
for our business, our readers and our planet. This book is made
from Forest Stewardship Council® certified paper.

To Emma

I got Covid.

I was in hospital for three months.

I was in a coma for 40 days and 40 nights. (Very biblical, I know, but I wasn't in charge. This book is not about me thinking that I'm Noah or Jesus.)

I was in intensive care for 48 days.

I was in a rehab hospital for three weeks.

Chapter 1

I'm alive

A stranger stops me in the street. He says, 'I'm so glad that you've recovered. You're alive!'

My first thought is, *That's very kind of him.* I don't know him, but I can see that he's interested enough – in me or something to do with me – to make the effort to stop and tell me that he's glad I'm alive. I'm glad I'm alive too. After all, I did try to die, but they – the doctors and nurses – wouldn't let me. So I thank him. A naughty thought crosses my mind as I do, which is to ask him, 'How do you know I'm alive? I could be a dybbuk.' (Dybbuk being the Yiddish word for a ghost.) My mind rushes on, thinking of a possible book: *The Dybbuk of Muswell Hill.* The main character is me, wandering about north London, spooking around the great grey gaunt walls of Alexandra Palace.

1

(Apologies for this kind of mind-wandering. I do a lot of it. I think it helps me to get better. More on that later.)

I thank my new-found friend and walk on.

Have I recovered? I ask myself. *Is that what I am now? Recovered?*

I check myself over:

The blood clots – gone, says the doc.

The eye – still foggy.

The ear – still muffled.

The toes – still numb.

The varicose veins and piles – not good.

The pinball twinges (as I call the cramps that ping around my body, lighting up each bit of me in turn) – still there.

The damned ingrown toenail caused by Covid whacking out my big toenail, which then grew back into my toe – still there.

Breathlessness – gone.

Weakness – mostly gone, and the weakness that's there could be just me being 75.

So, am I recovered? Or am I recover*ing*? Or have I plateaued? Reached a level where I'm as good as I can expect to be, before I get to the slow-down in the final run-in?

I continue to ponder this new state of being ... I'm not the same as I was, though in some ways I'm better. I do more stretching, for example. I like stretching. I think of myself as a cat. They're very good at stretching, and it's good for the body and spirit. But what about my mind? If I'm really honest, it's not great. I'm bothered, aren't I? I'm bothered about lots of things that come crowding in on me if I wake up in the night – which is most nights now. The 'tyranny of the night', I call it. I'm bothered that my illness happened at all. I think I was stupid to have caught Covid. Why didn't I cancel those school visits, the trips to see Arsenal play, the radio work in BBC studios? Why did I wait until the government told us to lock down? I could have stayed at home, isolating. Aha, I reason with myself, but I live with three other people, and they had temperatures and loss of taste before I did . . . So I soon realise that this is a dead-end line of thinking. But it still bothers me.

I'm also bothered that I am not who I was. That person seems to me to have been more frivolous, more certain, less fragile than the person I am now. But why am I talking about two people here: the person I was and the person I am? This is a nonsense. I am still that person, it's just that something big happened to change me. Big things happen to all of us. When I was 16, I went on a holiday to France on my own, and I think I became someone different. We often say things like, 'I'm a changed person', and that is part of being human, changing. So don't overdramatise it, Michael, by talking about two people. That's what I tell myself.

And yet I cling on to this idea that there was a Before state of mind; and there is this new state of mind, that is the After. There's a bit sandwiched in between, which for me was the time in hospital. That's the During. Maybe I should think of these as chapters. We go through life in chapters. The parts are separate but linked. The chapter I'm in at the moment, then, is the chapter where our hero feels stupid, frail, on edge (a bit edgy), and also *on* an edge, an edge where I could at any moment literally fall over (I left giddiness off that checklist earlier). I bump into the sides of tables and chairs. But it's also an edge at the top of a cliff that looks down into the Pool of Glum. I don't like admitting this. Not even to myself, let alone sharing it with anyone else. Yes, there are times that even though I can walk, talk, see, hear, feel, touch, and even though I have the loveliest family in the world, I have work that I love doing, and I have all the support and praise that anyone could ever want, there are times when I look over the edge of that cliff down into something full of loss.

Where does it come from? Why do I find myself on that cliff edge? Why do I look down? How much can a person – any person – cope with? We talk of 'stress' and 'strain'. They're good words. They suggest that we're like steel girders which can take weight and twist, but only up to a point. If you do too much to them, they bend, crack and break. I wonder what my cracking point is. Did I get near to it?

People talk to me about post-traumatic stress disorder. They say that people like me, who were in a coma in intensive care for several weeks (nearly seven for me), may well have a form of PTSD. I've listened to people who've come back from wars and heard how they've woken up in the night, bathed in sweat, screaming. Or how they've turned nasty and attacked people who love them and care for them. I don't think that's me, and yet I have what I call Lonely Corridor Syndrome. This is my name for a feeling that mixes loneliness, sadness and loss. It's connected to what feels like the sensation of something real: a place, a time, a smell, and yet it's no more than a vision, a kind of daydream.

Lonely Corridor Syndrome is where I am at one end of a long, empty corridor. It's a corridor that starts from where I am, perhaps in the loo in the middle of the night, and it links up with remembered lonely corridors in the hospital, and at school (I was often thrown out of class), or late at night at the university where I teach. The corridors link up, stretching away into the distance, with closed doors on either side, dimmed white lights overhead. (I like inventing syndromes. I've got at least two others: Alternate Day Syndrome, to describe how I exercise one day and flop out on the sofa the next; and Major Hollywood

5

Star Forgetting Syndrome. So far I've forgotten the names of Tom Cruise, George Clooney and Meryl Streep. I can live with this but it does mean that I'll never agree to go on *Pointless* again. I know that I would forget Elvis's name.)

I didn't used to get Lonely Corridor Syndrome. It's part of the new me. It's part of this person who is still bugged by what's happened to him. Sometimes I call it frailty. We know what frail means. We see our oldest relatives, stooping, struggling to walk or hold things. Medics talk about frail bones. Our whole constitution can be frail, and someone sneezing near us can cause our whole system to fail. Hey, wait a minute, that's probably what happened to me! Someone sneezed. The virus sprayed out of their nose at 90 miles an hour, and I walked into the damp cloud of their sneeze. The virus went into my nose and mouth, down into my lungs, into my blood, invaded the cells on the lining of arteries and veins, and soon I was getting clots and haemorrhages. My body rushed fluid and mucus to wherever things were breaking down and next thing I was in trouble: lungs, liver, kidneys, nerves, toes, brain . . .

So, I'm frail. Doctors, nurses, physiotherapists, occupational therapists – teams of people, squadrons, armies – saved me. I tried to die but they wouldn't let me. (That's the second time I've said this, isn't it? I repeat myself a lot these days. And I also repeat this to myself to remind me just how great it is that we invented this beautiful thing, the NHS, to do the most important thing in the world: fight for people's lives.)

But they left me with my frailty. Of course they did. They didn't abandon me. They made a judgement that got me to a point where whatever I did next was down to me. They had done their job. I was 'discharged', as they say. It took me a few weeks to stop thinking that every ache, every concern, belonged to them. You see, when you're 'inside', you are in a way owned by those doctors and nurses. They have reams of paper and computer files all about you. They stand round your bed and tell you that something is 58 per cent or 94 per cent. They even know what your insides look like because they've looked at the scans. Fancy that. They've seen bits of you that you've not even seen yourself. 'You've got a thymic cyst,' says one, 'but I'm pretty sure it's benign.' What?! A thymic cyst? Where? Why? I know I've got a mole on my right shoulder blade that I can't actually see, but a thymic cyst? Where is such a thing? Why do I have a cyst that is thymic? 'By the way, doctor, what is a thymic cyst?'

And the obs. Do you know about obs? You lie in bed and, after the nurse has done your blood pressure, pulse, temperature and oxygen take-up, they do your obs. They stand at the end of the bed and stare at you. At first, if you're not used to it, it can be quite disconcerting. A person you don't know, in uniform, is looking at you very hard, with a very still look on their face, for a whole minute. Not many people do this sort of thing in real life, so you're not really ready for it. It gets worse: at the end of the obs, they write something down. You wonder what they've written. That I need a shave? That I need to pull myself together and stop being dreary? That I should have rung my wife? They don't say. Just think about it. Somewhere in the bowels of a hospital in north London there are more than 60 days of obs all about me. Did they make a note of the wart in the middle of my forehead? Perhaps that wasn't important.

So, while you're in hospital, they own you. But then you come home. You're on your own. And you're still frail. What I learned was that I had to take this on. To make the frailty mine. My frailty had belonged to the doctors and nurses, but these people weren't at home with me. So I had to own my frailty. I couldn't deny it, and pretend that I was stronger than I was. I couldn't dump it on someone else, or try to make them as frail as me in the hope that it would relieve me of it. It was all mine and it was down to me to find ways to deal with it, to make it easier to carry, easier to own. That in itself was a way of owning it. Taking on the responsibility of dealing with it. Getting myself to the hospital, the optician, the foot clinic for the check-ups, getting out of the house to walk round the block to get the exercise, lifting the saucepan and walking round the kitchen to get the strength into my arms and core.

Owning your own frailty doesn't mean being defined by it. I am my frailty but I am also more than my frailty. No matter how much I moan to myself about how feeble or stupid or dreary I am, I am more than that. I am all the other things I do, things that are nothing whatsoever to do with having been sick, having been in a state where I couldn't stand up and couldn't walk. Watching *Strictly Come Dancing*, doing a Zoom talk to some children at the other end of the country, writing a poem, meeting up with my grownup children and a thousand other things – all are evidence to me that I am not defined by what's happened. It's worth reminding myself of that quite often.

All this has got me thinking about getting better: what it means, and how we do it.

In this book, you'll see me grappling with family loss, chronic illness, being sacked, lack of feeling, trying to feel good about education, being committed, paranoia, the death of my son Eddie, recovering from Covid and how I use writing to deal with it. Along the way, I hope to offer ways of coping that will be useful for you. I tell stories, because I think stories are a great way for us to compare ourselves with the story we read. The stories aren't commands or even recommendations. They are examples for you to chew on or, even better, blueprints for you to try out. I also discover and explore ways of thinking: self-blame and self-deception, naming things as a way of solving things, and finding the absurd in our moments of greatest difficulty.

I finish the book with a chapter called 'Raisins to be cheerful'. It sums up the advice I've given elsewhere. And no, 'raisins' is not a misprint. Raisins make me happy: finding the things that make you happy can help you get better.

I hope it helps.

Chapter 2

Alan

I'm sitting with my brother and father. I'm about ten, so my brother is 14 and our father must be in his late thirties. (Really? That young? How could someone who seemed so knowledgeable, clever, capable and in charge have been so young?)

We are going through old photos. They're in a shirt box, lying loose and jumbled up. We pull them out one by one – who's that? Where's that? We have favourites: the one where our father and mother are walking down a street eating ice creams. It's summer and Mum is wearing big flappy shorts. Our father looks like an athlete in his running vest. Well, he was an athlete. A bus passes by in the background as they walk along, smiling forever.

There are pictures of his own father – Morris – who he never saw again after his mother gathered him up, along with his sister and baby brother, and brought them from Brockton, Massachusetts to England on the SS *President Harding*. And there are piles of photos from the camping holidays that we go on in Wales, Yorkshire, Northumberland, Brittany, the Jura Mountains and the Pyrenees. We're big on camping in our family. Our parents are teachers: they grab those five-week summer holidays with both hands and we live all that time in tents. They seem to think being wet and cold – or baking hot in the south of France – along with digging and using latrines does us good. Our father sounds proud as he answers our questions and fills in details. Then we pull out a picture of Mum with a baby on her knee. I ask Dad whether it is me or my brother, Brian. He looks at it. He looks even closer. He says, 'It isn't you or Brian. It's Alan. He died.'

This was the first time that either Brian or I had ever heard of Alan. There had been no mention of him from either of our parents, nor from close relatives or family friends. There were no pictures of him in the house, there was no memorial or grave that we knew of and we had never come across any books with giveaway dedications. He had disappeared without trace, until this moment.

I can remember the moment clearly. I was sitting on the floor. Our father was in a chair. We were in our 'front room' in our first-floor flat that overlooked the street. There was something about the way our father spoke of sad or lost things, they would settle on us like snow. We would go quiet, not knowing what to say. It irritated Mum, who would always say that he shouldn't be like this. If he told us about 'The Trunk', a beloved possession that his mother left behind in a flat that she moved out of, he would tell the story with the same regretful, helpless voice that he was using now with the photo of Alan. And Mum would say, 'It's gone. There's no use going on about it. It's gone. Why do you always go on and on about it?'

But Mum wasn't in the room when we found the photo, so our father was able to say it how he wanted to. One of us asked, 'How did he die?' He answered directly, 'Whooping cough. I was away in the army, in Frankfurt or Berlin, and he coughed himself to death in your mother's arms. The war was still on and they didn't have the medicines.'

This must be the first time that I had a sense that grief and loss are handled in different ways by different people. I saw it in that moment, but I've only really figured it out over the years: my father wanting to say something, my mother wanting to say nothing. And that strange invisibility of Alan. Thinking about it now, all these years after, it really does seem odd.

Somewhere in the back of my mind I realised that what had happened to our father was a rerun of what had happened to his mother. Not long after she arrived in England with her three children, the youngest, a baby, died. In the space of a few months, two children lost both their father and a baby brother. The family story was that the father, Morris, back in Brockton, was angry and blamed his wife for losing the baby. Then, as the years rolled by and he didn't ever follow her to England, the story was that he never forgave her. In the cramped two-up two-down terrace house in Whitechapel, full of his mother's sisters and brother and parents, our father dreamed that one day his American dad would arrive and say, 'Harold, I'm here. Let me take you away from all this.' But he didn't ever come. He died in the Boston Mental Hospital, known locally as the Mattapan. Years later, our father and I met people who did know Morris: American cousins. They had stories about him, how he spoke in trade union meetings, how he had five suits and a convertible, how secretly he had what they called 'an illegitimate child' with the person they called 'the landlady in Rochester', and how he was buried in the Jewish Workmen's Circle Cemetery in Melrose, Massachusetts, and how on the grave it said, 'Morris Rosen, beloved father'.

I'm running to and fro across decades here, aren't I? I've come to realise that that's how we think. We don't think in a neat, orderly, chronological order. Later things land on earlier things and mingle with them. Things that come later can sometimes explain things that come earlier. And I'm on the floor looking at the picture of Alan right now, 65 years later, and I'm wondering why our father never mentioned him before. Why was there no evidence of him in our flat? No marks, no signs of him having ever lived? Why had no one else mentioned him? Had they been sworn to secrecy? If so, why? Why should a death be secret?

But then there's a bigger mystery: Mum. As I said, she wasn't in the room as we looked at the photo. Well, in a way, she was. She was in the photo – Alan was sitting on her knee – but of course that doesn't count. She is just a photographic presence in my memory. Despite Brian and I finding out about Alan, Mum never mentioned him to us, ever. That's about 20 years of silence from us finding the photo until she died in 1976. I can't even be absolutely sure that our father told her about the conversation, but I think it's very likely. They seemed to be people who shared everything to do with my brother and me. In fact, they chewed over the rights and wrongs of the ways of the world so much that it's hard for me not to believe that Mum's silence was agreed on and carried out according to some principle or other. I don't know what that principle would be, other than that there's a good chance it was as much of a principle as the motions they liked to pass in union and Communist Party branch meetings.

I should say that our father did sometimes drop Alan's name into conversations for the rest of his life, but only when Mum wasn't in the room, and in the decades he lived after she died. It would only be a quick mention, nothing dwelled on, and not clothed in any detail. And I never got any sense of how they coped, what people said to them, who helped them. If I concentrate very hard, I can remember a rumour that our father's sister had offered to have a baby for our parents – but can that be true? They were in their twenties. Had they said that they didn't want to have any more children? But hang on, they did. Me! My brother was born in 1942, too young to remember Alan, who was born in 1944, and I was born in 1946.

I'm the baby who came after. Was I, then, the baby who helped them get better? Was I part of the reason why Alan didn't get mentioned? I was perhaps the new beginning, the turned-over new leaf. I'll imagine it. They were delighted to have a new baby to think about. By the time I was a few months old, our father was home for good from the army and didn't have to trundle to and fro from Germany, strapped to the wooden struts in old Dakota cargo planes. Apart from the chunks of US Army gear that he took with him on those camping holidays, he put all that behind him too. The post-war years were for putting a lot of things behind them.

But we're Jewish.

There were others who were spoken of in the same way as our father had spoken of Alan: the French uncles. Every now and then, even with Mum in the room, our father would say, 'I had two French uncles, you know. They were there at the beginning of the war but they weren't there at the end.' The same look on his face, the dropped, floppy cheeks, the downward slope of the eyes, the descending run of his voice. And the same annoyed comeback from Mum: 'Why do you go on about these things?'

Once or twice, when we were children, either I or my brother would say, 'What happened to them?' And our father would say, 'They must have died in the camps.' What did that mean? Which camps? Where? We didn't get a TV until 1957, and there were no books in the house about Nazi Germany or the Holocaust. I can remember my mother's brother and parents, my father's mother and sisters, our parents' many Jewish friends, but I don't remember any of them talking about 'the camps' before I was in my teens.

So here was another part of our family that was supposed to be untouchable, but that either my father or us kids would occasionally worry at, a bit like that hole in your gum after the dentist has taken out a tooth. There was a handful of little facts that went

17

with the uncles: they were Morris's brothers. One was called Martin, the other Oscar. One was a dentist, one was a clock mender. They lived in eastern France, maybe Nancy, maybe Metz, maybe Strasbourg. They had all started out in Poland.

At the time, I didn't know anyone else who had these kinds of shadows in their family. I think now that's because they weren't talking about it either. If I line up my mother's relatives or the Jewish friends: Moishe, Rene, Chick, Gertrude, Dinah, Bertha, Solly, Vic, Rosa, Lily, Harry . . . I don't remember chats in that front room where they talked of lost relatives. If they did, it was out of earshot of us children. It was not to be shared with us, perhaps. Was there some kind of agreement between them all to not mourn? To move on? To get better by getting on?

There were two exceptions to this. In 1957, we went to Germany. Let me quickly say that I don't remember this being any kind of problem for my parents. Later, I got to know the parents of my Jewish friends from school and they would say that they would never buy a German car. But we headed off to Weimar in East Germany in 1957 and mostly our holiday was full of trips to famous houses and factories – Goethe's house, Schiller's house, the Wartburg car factory, the Jena lens factory and so on. But one day our parents said that they were going somewhere we couldn't go too. It was, they said, somewhere too awful. It was called Buchenwald. When they came back that evening, my mother was shaken. The skin under her eyes was drawn and dark. She said that terrible things had gone on in Buchenwald. Thousands of people had been tortured and murdered. I was 11 – I'm not sure that I made the clear connection between other conversations that Mum had with us and this visit. Mum would often spend teatimes telling us about 'the war'. She used the salt and pepper pots, plates and dishes to tell us about doodlebugs, the Battle of Stalingrad, the march on Berlin, Hitler in his bunker. In these chats, she would often tell us that if Hitler had got to Britain we wouldn't be alive and the reason for this was that we were Jews. So I knew about it, but in a way there was a lot of not-knowing. Why was that?

I think it's because, again, they thought that this is how you get better: say as little as possible about these terrible things. But then with the visit to Buchenwald, for a moment, the curtain lifted, and I could see that my mother was disturbed, unhappy, distressed. Yet, because I hadn't been allowed to go, the whole affair was also full of mystery and hidden ghastliness. They were, after all, trying to protect us, not burden us with this thing that had happened that we couldn't do anything about. Was that it?

Our trip to Germany ended in Berlin. On one of our days out, an older woman in the German group we were with took us to Unter den Linden. Before the war this had been a beautiful boulevard, but was now nothing. I remember the flattened buildings and rubble on either side of the street. 'Hitler loved linden trees,' the woman said, more to herself than us. This flipped Mum's switch. She turned to my father and said in a furious whisper, 'I don't bloody care what Hitler liked! Why is she telling us this?' My father – ever the diplomat – tried to quieten her down. I looked from one to the other and back again. Why was she so cross? Why had this single comment made her so angry? I couldn't answer this at the time. I can now, of course. These moments tell me that a lot more was bubbling under the surface than we ever talked about openly.

Throughout my teens, things became clearer, documentaries appeared on the TV that we now had. I also had Jewish friends at school who talked about 'the camps', and there was one bizarre guy in our group who had some kind of obsession with the Nazis. He would strut about pretending to be Hitler or Himmler as though he were some kind of comedy act. He would draw tanks and Messerschmitts and rows of German soldiers marching across his exercise books. He even did weird impressions of camp guards stubbing out cigarettes on imaginary victims' faces.

What was this about? Why did he do it? Why did we let him do it? And why did we laugh? I think of this as a tiny vignette of how a group of boys in the London suburbs of the early 1960s, some Jewish, some not, were handling the horrors that were being slowly revealed to us, horrors that had taken place less than 20 years earlier. I don't think we helped ourselves one bit. We ended up turning it into some kind of burlesque, with the Nazi leadership as clowns. On one occasion, Mum overheard me and a friend imitating the boy with the obsession and she did something that was rare for her: she got very angry with me. She reminded me that what had happened was very real and that millions had died. That shut me up. Joke over. Again, Mum had revealed that there was an underground pool of rage and sorrow that connected all these things.

Around this time, my cousin got married. At the wedding, my father pointed out a man who he said was his cousin. You may well ask why I hadn't ever met my father's cousin before, but you may also know that families are strange places and that who meets up with whom or who does not meet with whom can be long and complicated stories. Anyway, this was the first time I had ever seen this man – also called Michael – who was my father's cousin. He's Polish, they explained. His mother was Morris's Polish sister, in other words, my father's aunt.

The story that the family told me about this cousin at the wedding was that his parents had put him – aged about 16 or 17 – on a train in western Poland to escape the Nazis. He had gone to eastern Poland, where the Russians were. The Russians had put him in a labour camp, where he worked till the Nazis invaded eastern Poland and Russia too. Then he joined the Polish Free Army, marched and fought down to Iran and on to Palestine, then north to Italy, where he fought at the terrible Battle of Monte Cassino. Then he had come to England, had been in some kind of camp here, and had fetched up on my father's sister's doorstep some time in the late 1940s. He never saw his parents again.

Even as a teenager, I had some sense that this Michael was a survivor. I thought of what it must have been like to say goodbye to your parents, at around the age I was then, and never see them again. I don't think I did much with that thought, other than to think it. Looking back, I can see that all these fragments sit in my mind, doing the job of telling me about the fragility of humankind, in particular the corner of humankind my family belonged to in the 1930s and 40s. The only ones who were safe were in the US and Britain. With just one shift in the balance of power, any of us could have gone the way the French and Polish ones did.

I think it's odd the way my parents handled all this. I can find words to describe it, and can understand their motives. They were trying to shield us from the pain. In my mother's case, both with her own child and with these stories, she had a philosophy that said, 'What can you do? Nothing. So if there's nothing you can do, why go on about it?'

By the time I was a student at university several years later, things had taken a few more twists. I had stayed in France on my own, in a summer camp in the Ardèche. One night we went up to 'the plateau' and had stumbled across a memorial in the dark. We shone torches at it, and it told in its bleak, abbreviated way that members of the Resistance had been shot on that spot. My French companions cursed and spat. For the first time, even though we had spent several of those camping holidays in France, I was face to face with something to do with my father's uncles. I wrote home to tell him about it. I was, in an unknowing way, moving from my mother's position of letting sleeping dogs lie to wanting to think more about these horrors that had taken place before I was born.

This came into sharp focus when I was at home from university and my father and I stayed up late at night to watch the two parts of an extraordinary and troubling film by Marcel Ophuls, *Le Chagrin et la Pitié* (*The Sorrow and the Pity*). The documentaries tell the story of the Nazi occupation of France, the Resistance, the collaboration, and the deportation of Jews out of France to Auschwitz and other camps. I remember my father saying, 'This is what must have happened to my uncles.'

Again, there's not a lot even a 20-year-old can do with that. And so it stayed at the back of my mind, until I was in my forties and I decided to go to America and knit together some of the bits of the Rosen family that had once been strewn across the Western world from Poland to France, from England to the US.

This is what I pieced together: I found the police report of how one uncle – Martin – had been arrested in the middle of the night in 1943, and handed over to the Nazis. I found the regional Nazi Kommandant's edict that all Jews should be rounded up, and the prefect's report – with names – showing that he had done just that. I discovered that Martin, Polish by birth, had fought in the Foreign Legion on the side of the French in the First World War and had been naturalised in 1923. This was no protection for him. He was deported from Paris to Auschwitz and never returned.

I found that the other uncle – Oscar – had married someone called Rachel, and they fled to western France as the German army invaded. When the net closed round Jews, with the requirement that they wear yellow stars, mark their market stalls with 'Entreprise Juive' (Jewish business), and that their belongings be 'aryanised' – that is, handed over to the state – Oscar and Rachel had fled to Nice, where the Italians were protecting Jews. A philanthropist requisitioned four boats and was on the verge of helping the Jews escape to newly liberated North Africa when the Western Allies defeated Italy. The philanthropist pleaded with General Eisenhower to not announce the armistice, in order to give him time to get the Jews out to safety, but Eisenhower went ahead anyway. A few days later, the Nazis marched into Nice. Many Jews were waiting in requisitioned hotels and the Nazis rounded them up, transported them to Paris and deported them to Auschwitz. Amongst them were Oscar Rosen and his wife Rachel. Oscar had fought on the side of the Germans in the First World War in a Polish regiment. The two brothers had fought on opposite sides. Later, I found out that Martin had been the best man at Oscar's wedding.

That story took me 30 years to put together. When I got to the end of it, I thought I had got to the end of everything. There was one more twist. When the oldest of my father's American cousins died, aged 103, he left behind a locked closet. His son opened it up. In the closet was a sealed box, labelled 'Family Photos'. He opened the box. In it were photos of Martin, Oscar and Rachel, along with the Polish relatives too. I remembered I had sat in that room with the locked closet, asking my father's cousin if he had known anything at all about Oscar and Martin. No, he'd said, no more than I already knew. I asked his sister the same question. She remembered, she said, writing to one of the French cousins in order to practise her school French. Did she still have those letters? No, she said. Later, I found that that same cousin (niece of Oscar and Martin) had applied to US Immigration to get Oscar out of France. Why didn't they tell me about any of this?

Amongst the photos in the locked closet there was one picture of my father's cousin Michael (remember him, from the wedding and the Polish Free Army?) walking down a street in western Poland arm in arm with his mother (Stella Rechnic, née Rosen) and his aunt, Bella Rosen. I was able to get the picture to Michael – then in his nineties – and he had never seen it before. It was only the second picture of his mother that he had. He was 'mesmerised', his son told me.

So here are other stories about getting better: my father's American cousins physically hiding what they knew of those who were killed; me spending 30 years (on and off, I hasten to add) trying to piece together the narrative of how these Rosens had died. In our very different ways we were trying to solve things, trying to deal with horrors that on one level were highly personal and familial and on the other were social, national, global even. The generation before me tried to look forward, bury the past, get on with it, build warm, comfortable, safe lives. In the case of the American end of the family, I'm going to guess there was some guilt that they couldn't get their uncles out.

But for me, not knowing what had happened to my father's relatives was infuriating. It nagged at me because it felt like the Nazis had not only got away with removing them but had succeeded in extinguishing their memory. They had simply vanished, and that hurt. Doing the research and finding out what happened was, in its own small way, a means of pushing back against that painful sense that the Nazis had won. It was almost a relief, if a somewhat selfish one.

One moment in particular stands out. The local authority covering where Martin was arrested opened up their archives and I applied for any papers that mentioned him. Very quickly, a set of documents came back, including the police report filed by four gendarmes the morning after they'd rounded him up. In very matter-of-fact language, it recounts how they called at the house of Madame Bobières at 2.30am and arrested a man called Martin Rozen (he spelled it the Polish way), 1.62 metres tall, with a scar on his face, wearing a cotton jacket and trousers, flat shoes, and a Basque beret. It was utterly chilling to read this official paper, lodged on the morning after an event that was just one moment in a whole genocide. I sometimes imagine those four policemen doing what policemen do when they come off duty – perhaps having a coffee and croissant and chatting about their night's work. It surprises me every time I think about it, how ordinary and official this event is. Tough and cruel and indifferent as it all seems, though, there is some kind of satisfaction for me that I've found these last traces of someone in our family who otherwise would have been invisible.

But what was I doing, spending all that time and energy? In one sense it's absurd. I can't bring anyone back to life. Most of the story I found out after my father had died, so I wasn't even filling in the gaps for him. In any case, the bits that I found out before he died were either too painful or too distant for him to be interested in them. Clearly, if this was doing anything for anyone, it was doing it for me. It was helping me deal with that look on my father's face when he told me about Alan, and told me about 'the two French uncles'. It had felt like filling a gap, a hole bigger than the lost trunk that his mother left behind, and connecting with a horror which I had discovered was a horror at the heart of the whole of humanity. How had this happened – scientific, industrialised genocide – in the core of Western civilisation? In my own tiny way, in our corner, I had found some descriptions and perhaps one or two explanations, particularly in that chain of command from the regional Kommandant, to the local Prefect, to the local gendarmes.

I hardly dare say that there was a satisfaction in my doing this, but there was. I feel glad to have put to bed the nagging feeling of not knowing. And I'm glad to know that when – and this really has happened – I stand up somewhere and someone says, 'Yeah, but none of this happened, did it?', I can show them the documents and the photos and say, 'It did.'

It can also take me somewhere special. Every five years, the Shoah Memorial in Paris holds a series of commemorations for each 'convoy' that shipped Jews out of France to be killed. Oscar was on Convoy 62, Martin was on Convoy 68. I went to Paris for each commemoration, stood up at the front of all the other relatives of deportees and read out the names of my father's uncles and aunt. The custom was also to read on down the list of names until we reached the next name who had a relative present at the ceremony. This entailed reading out some ten or more names. 'Say the ages of the children,' the usher whispered to me. So not only did I read out Oscar Rosen and Martin Rozen, but I read out the names of children as young as five.

This felt like a ritual. I haven't done many rituals in my life, but here was a moment that felt totally right. I was in a hall with people each with a similar story of the totally unjust, cruel, genocidal elimination of people in their families, each one with a long tail of sorrow stretching down from the 1940s to now. We didn't sing or pray or give speeches. The names were enough: over a thousand of them, once living people crammed into cattle trucks, pulling out of Paris, heading east.

The village where Martin was arrested has also done something extraordinary: the Mayor is a history teacher and, once he heard from me what had happened in his village in 1944, he took his students to Paris to see Martin's name on the Wall of Names at the Shoah Memorial. More: the council decided to engrave Martin's name on the village war memorial and name the local park after him. All this is a big deal, because the way the story of the Second World War is told in France is much disputed and very political. For the village to commemorate what happened there nearly 80 years ago feels very special.

On 8 May 2022, we visited the village for the ceremony they hold every year to commemorate the 'fallen'. The village band was playing, all the flags were out, there were men in uniform – former soldiers, the local police, the firemen. The mayor stepped forward to make a speech, and asked me to stand beside him.

In the first part of his speech he told the story of how Martin Rozen fought in the First World War, was injured, lived in Metz and then in the village during the Second World War. He told how Martin was arrested on the night of 31 January 1944, right here in the village, and then deported to Auschwitz. I stood in the sun listening to this with everyone else and it felt very much as if a circle was being closed – that I had done what I wanted to do: find a way of putting Martin Rozen back into a living community. Later, the Mayor showed me the house where he was living on the night he was arrested; he told me a story of how there was a woman he worked with who remembered him from when she was a school-girl. She would look out of her window and see him cross the road to go to Le Cheval Blanc (The White Horse), a restaurant in the village, to get his meals. The plan is to name the village park 'Le Parc Martin Rosen' with a plaque and panels to tell the story of what happened.

The Mayor explained that whatever this meant to me, part of his reason for doing all this was political. Some young people had daubed swastikas on a public building. There had been quite a strong vote in the village – not a majority – for the anti-immigrant presidential candidates, including some for the candidate who had explicitly tried to excuse France for its role in the deportation of Jews. The ceremony had been a reply. I felt good about that.

In a way, my father had got it right when he guessed that his uncles had 'died in the camps', but it was so inconclusive and without detail that it felt all the more unjust for it. Our relatives, (our 'meshpukhe' in Yiddish), had been vanished. And wasn't this part of the Nazi project anyway? Not only to exterminate but to drive the memory that we existed out of European history? By spending all that time retrieving lists, edicts and reports out of archives I had defeated that aim. I was saying, 'You will not remove us from history.'

Now that felt as good as anything that could be described as 'good' in this saga. I hadn't reversed anything, I hadn't saved anyone, but I had made a contour of history clear. In my own way, I had also replied to my mother's philosophy about moving on, not dwelling on regrets about the past because, according to her, there was nothing you could do about it. Actually, I realised I had done something to do with the past and I felt better for doing so.

I'm wary of advising or telling other people what to do. What I'm doing here is talking about myself (and to myself!). My method in this is to lay things that I've been through in front of you, and give you my thoughts about them. They're not instructions, though. And they're not blueprints for how you should behave. They are for you to do what you want with them – use them, adapt them, reject them, in order to think up your own ways of dealing with things.

Chapter 3

Technically, you're dead

I am sitting in a small room in Barts Hospital in London. This is the renal department – stuff to do with kidneys. Sitting in front of me is Mr Baker. He is brisk but calm. He has my notes in front of him. I've had a blood test and my GP has referred me to Mr Baker because he suspects that my kidneys are failing. I had already been to see my GP about my eyes. They leaked. Yes, everyone 'tears up' a bit when a cold wind blows, but my eyes, I told him, seem to leak all the time. At first he thought it was conjunctivitis and gave me some sticky yellow ointment to squeeze into them. I did that for two weeks but nothing changed. I went back and this time he considered my kidneys. After a blood test, he told me that my haemoglobin looked a bit dodgy too. When he looked at my leaky eyes, he asked me if my eyelids had always been pink and swollen. I said that I didn't know.

Now I was with Mr Baker. He stopped looking from the notes and back to me and, instead, seemed to take off in another direction. He asked me what I had been doing this week. I told him that I had been out with some school students from George Green Comprehensive School on the Isle of Dogs, exploring the landscape with a view to writing poems. They had spotted a dead creature floating in the water of the disused dock. Was it a dog? A fox? Or something else? I told him about one young lad being amused by the fact that on the coach I had sung a jingle for a kids' toy: 'Weebles wobble but they don't fall down.' From then on, he called me Weeble. In fact, from that time, the whole group called me Weeble.

Mr Baker pushed the notes to one side. 'I think this is all rubbish,' he said. He paused, and then said something that changed my life.

Now let's go back to before Mr Baker, before leaking eyes and sticky yellow ointment. I'm going to set out a list of things, but before I do, I'll explain to you that this is cheating. At any time in our lives, our bodies have stuff going on that we think of as not being quite right. Sometimes there may be two, three or more things at any given moment. If these things are very different, or at different ends of our body, there may be no reason why we untrained non-medical people would connect them. A list, though, does connect them. I am writing 40 years after my visit to Mr Baker in Renal, so from the vantage point of now, I can connect them. In the ten to 12 years pre-Baker, these were disconnected oddities going on in and around different parts of my body and mind. Sometimes they would bother me. Sometimes I would be sadly curious, sometimes bewildered or numb. As each one of these 'conditions' made themselves known to me, I reacted. I adjusted my mind, which made me adapt to what was going on. It was as if I met each one with a shrug: 'Well, that's me.' Some doctors would say that the shrug is one of the symptoms of the illness anyway!

I'll start with me noticing one day, about 12 years before seeing Mr Baker, that the backs of my hands were puffy. If you clench your fist, most of you will be able to see your knuckles, with the bones showing under the skin. For most of us, if we make the shape of a tiger's claw with our hands, we might also see lines running from our wrist towards the knuckles. On this day, over a decade before sticky, yellow ointment day, I noticed puffiness. I worked out what it was: I had been bitten by a gnat or flea the day before. Probably. (See what I did there? I explained it away.) Sure enough, the puffiness seemed to go away. Mostly. (There I go again! It didn't go away entirely but I told myself that it had 'mostly' gone away. More explaining something so that it's not a bother, not making me anxious. It's like making a shield to protect yourself.)

Here's another symptom: on a cold day in winter, I was on a coach. Instead of feeling cold, I noticed that I had started clenching my whole body. My teeth locked and I felt my ribs ache. I hugged myself, rubbed my legs, drummed my feet on the coach floor, but whatever I did, I had this frozen ache across my chest. I must have a bit of a temperature, I thought. (More explaining! You see what I was doing there: using bits of knowledge about how and why we feel cold. I knew, of course, about the way we shudder and clench when we have a temperature, and decided that was what happened on that coach journey. This sorted it, and I put it in a box and tucked it away in the back of my mind where it wouldn't trouble me.)

One day, when I was at university, the photographer for the student newspaper came to take pictures of me. He got me to stand under the very studenty light I had in my room. When he sent me the photos, I thought how strange it was that I had such big bags under my eyes, and yet I was only 21. I worked out what it was: staying up too late. A few months later, I noticed that these bags could sometimes get itchy and annoying. *I must get to bed earlier*, I thought. And yet these things made me sad. Thinking about it now, this was the starting point of a growing cloud of sadness, with the cloud gathering as each 'condition' appeared. Being sad is in its way a coping mechanism, but an ineffectual one. It's a kind of resignation, almost a form of self-blame. Being sad was a way of sending a message to myself to do nothing. In fact, thinking about it now makes me sad all over again.

On we go: around this same time, I attended a lot of student meetings. I spoke at some of them, and noticed that there were times when I was very clear but others when I sounded, to myself at least, stumbly. 'Furry', I called it. It annoyed me and worried me. *More late nights*, I thought. I was using my mother's lines of advice to me! 'You need sleep. You get ill if you don't sleep.' That's something else we do: talk to ourselves with the voices of our parents. They're in our heads and we use them either to agree or violently disagree. I sometimes say that my mum (or dad) is a 'map', sitting in my head laying out routes, telling me where to go. I don't have to obey, but the maps are there all the same.

I liked to go running. I didn't use a stopwatch so I didn't measure my times, but I noticed that there were occasions when I felt as if I was running through porridge. I couldn't move my legs fluently. Other times it was fine. I started to look out for these porridge moments. Mostly they came when I was running up any kind of slope. Late nights again? This was the kind of thing that would leave me with questions, often rising up in front of my eyes as I went to sleep. Why did my legs feel like porridge today? There was the silence of no answer. As I dozed off, the question would ask itself over and over again, firing off into a blankness. As there was no answer in my mind, I resolved that there was literally no answer. I decided that these 'conditions' were inevitable, and that was a strong reason to do nothing about them.

On another occasion, I was beating some eggs. Omelettes and scrambled eggs were the first meals that I learned how to cook. I liked beating eggs. I liked my omelettes. Why though, on this particular day, were the muscles in my forearm seizing up? I could hear the beat of the fork in the bowl slowing down. From my aborted medical course, I remembered something called 'summation', something to do with muscles reaching a maximum level of stimulation, beyond which they don't have time to relax. Instead of contracting and relaxing, they go into a permanent state of contraction. This was happening to me and my omelette. Must be an age thing, I thought. I am 23, after all. Getting on a bit. A word for that is 'rationalisation' – coming up with good, logical reasons for something even though the good, logical reasons are complete rubbish for the thing you're thinking about.

I met up with Toby, an old friend from university. We swapped jokes, did 'take-offs' of old friends, reminisced about plays we had been in together and parted, vowing to meet up again soon. A few weeks later, my girlfriend said to me that she had bumped into Toby and he had asked her if I was on drugs. 'Mike's speech was slurred,' he said, 'he seemed confused.' He remembered me as someone very speedy, and hadn't my voice got deeper? It sounded kind of gruff. I listened to all this and felt annoyed and resentful. Things weren't going great between me and the girlfriend, so was she getting at me? One cause of tension between us was that she always wanted to do stuff, go out, go for a walk, and I was mostly happy sitting hunched over a book. Now, it was as if she had got backup from Toby. I was probably tired, I thought. My speech slurred? Of course it's not drugs. I had never (have never) taken any drugs, other than those prescribed by doctors, and have hardly ever drunk alcohol. Why did Toby think I was on drugs? It upset me.

These 'conditions' were starting to be part of my emotional life with others; my relationships, in other words. There was a complicated knot in my head made up of wanting to deny what Toby had said was true, explaining it as my girlfriend's irritation with me, hunkering down into myself, somehow justifying it as my personality or me being 'the way I am' and resenting the fact that people wanted to change me. And yet also in the knot was that background sadness: something had changed and I didn't know why. And – strangely, you might say – it didn't seem medical. It seemed lifestyle-ish, something to do with a choice of behaviour. And yet, still, I couldn't do anything about it. Are you getting the picture of me becoming snarled up, tangled in a web?

At this time I was doing occasional BBC Schools broadcasts. I nearly always had the same produder, Joan, who had also produced my mother's programmes. Joan backed me, believed in me, encouraged me to write poems. She got me to write linking scripts between the poems and then come into the studio to record them. After every recording, I noticed that she would come out of 'the gallery', as it's called, into the studio and tell me to do it again. She would say things like, 'It's very slow today, Michael. Do you need some tea? Have you had enough to eat?' Was I slow, I wondered? It didn't feel slow to me. Another time, Joan said that I sounded 'mournful' and this would be off-putting for the children. Mournful? Me? Really? I'm not a mournful guy. Didn't people say of me that I was good company? How come I now sounded mournful? Again, you can't go to the doctors to tell them, 'People say that I sound mournful, doctor.' Instead, I made great efforts to speed up and sound cheery. I wondered why Joan was being so critical. Was it something I said? Had I annoyed her? Afterwards, I wondered how I had suddenly become a slow speaker. Didn't people used to say that I was speedy? I put this 'condition' into the sad box, and tried to forget about it.

I was working in a school in Vauxhall in south London. It was a girls' comprehensive school where a majority of the students were either from the Caribbean or were the children of Caribbean parents. The staff were focussed and committed to doing the best by the students. This was the first time that I had ever spent time, day after day, with people with a strong Caribbean heritage. As I was working in the field of poems and stories, this heritage was a constant theme, coming up in memories, jokes, songs, sayings, dialect, accents, talk about food, hairstyle, religion, folklore. There was a frankness about the way the students talked that I enjoyed.

One day, one of them said to me, 'You aren't half white.' I said to her, 'Well, I am white.' She looked closely at my face. 'No, *really* white though.' Was I whiter than Jim, head of English, or my friends Stephen and John, all of whom are also white? I hadn't noticed, but then, come to think of it, I hadn't noticed whiteness before. Why wouldn't someone of Caribbean origin be more sensitised to slight differences in whiteness? 'And another thing,' she said, 'are you on drugs?' 'No!' I said. 'I've never taken anything!' She looked doubtful. 'You have, though, innit?' I insisted I'd taken absolutely nothing, which was the truth.

This was the second time that someone thought I was on drugs, but why? It got through to me. Here, after all, was someone with no agenda with me (as the now-ex had, I thought) telling me the same thing. What was it about the way I looked or the way I spoke that made people think I took drugs? *I can't go to the doctors and say, 'People think I sound like I'm on drugs.'* I thought once again. *It's not a symptom, like loss of sight or night sweats.*

A year or so later, I was in another school, a boys' comprehensive this time. One student was in a lot of trouble and I found myself in a room with him, trying to help him write something. While the class teacher was occupied with someone else, he pulled a face that I could tell was a mockery of me. He pointed at my lips, pouted his lips and then rolled his bottom lip over so that this lip looked puffed and thick. I stared at him. I felt hurt. Why would he pick on something physical about me, and mock it? Then I remembered that the bunch of boys I was in with when I was at school had done precisely that. This is the cruelty of teenagers faced with anything that they (we) thought could be picked on and ridiculed. And now it was happening to me. But what was it with the lips? Were my lips puffy? This boy clearly thought so.

Later, I looked in the mirror. I pouted and stretched my lips. *Maybe I've become slack-jawed*, I thought. *I should do lip exercises to tighten up my lips*. I had started to feel ashamed of what I looked like, looking at myself in the mirror and wondering whether I had always been this way, whether my lips had always been that shape. I really did think that I could make my lips better and did sometimes stand in front of the mirror stretching my jaw, kidding myself that it would improve things. It was laughable and slightly tragic in the circumstances. A bit pathetic, really.

On another occasion, a photographer came to take photos of me for the cover of a book. When I came to look at them, I thought how strange it was that my hair had become frizzy. Didn't it used to be curly? Now it's straight, hard and coarse. And a slightly different colour. *Well*, I thought, *these things change across your life, and there's nothing I can do about it*. 'Nothing you can do about that': it's a theme that runs through all this. In its own way, it helps you cope. If you can't do anything about it, you can tell yourself that you just have to get on as if it isn't happening. An admirable thought in its own way, but not if it's leading to your own self-destruction.

Later, we were on holiday in Wales. It was Easter and there were two families sharing a cottage. We had a fire on inside. Every day, the idea was that we would go out for walks. But I found myself making excuses – I didn't really fancy it; it was too cold; I'd stay behind to make sure the fire was in. A few weeks after the holiday, we all met up again, and John from the other family said, 'Hah, and you spent the whole holiday by the fire!' *Did I?* I thought. *I know I looked after the fire a bit but was I really by the fire all the time? That seems a bit hard on me. After all, I'm 34, getting on a bit, so it's OK that I feel the cold, isn't it? Or am I ill?*

Yes, I did rationalise it that way. I really did put myself on the scrapheap at 34. I'm horrified by this, thinking back to it, but I know it's what I thought then. But all of these things had accumulated, and I was now, for the first time, beginning to think that something was really wrong. And I did feel bad that I couldn't be part of ordinary family fun like going for walks. So, I was no longer just sad – now I felt bad, too.

I was also struggling physically. I went for a walk with a friend on Hackney Marshes. It was tough going. I said, 'I'm OK on the flat, it's the hills that get me.' For the record, there are no hills on this bit of Hackney Marshes. This became a joke. 'Michael says there are hills on Hackney Marshes', 'The day that Michael thought there were hills on Hackney Marshes'. Everyone thought that was very funny. I tried to find it funny too. *Well, I am 35 now, so what do you expect?* Some of those slopes were just tough going for someone of my age . . .

But then came the leaky eyes, and the blood tests at the GP's, and Mr Baker in Renal.

He's pushed the notes to one side and told me that they're 'rubbish'. He looks very hard at my face and says, 'You're hypothyroid.'

The moment he said the word, my mind shot back nearly 20 years to two photos sitting on a page in a medical textbook. For two years, I had been on the path to becoming a doctor. In the end I changed direction, but there were bits and pieces in my mind from that time, like pieces of furniture in a junk shop, including those photos. The first photo showed a woman with a wide, puffed, moon-like face with drooping eyelids. The second, looking nothing like the first, was the same woman (with a long, bony face, bright eyes and curly hair). The text underneath explained that the woman on the left was someone suffering from hypothyroidism and the woman on the right was that same woman having received a few months of replacement therapy. That is, after receiving a daily dose of one of the hormones that the thyroid gland produces.

I realised the moment Mr Baker said 'You're hypothyroid' that I was the woman on the left. I saw in my mind a photo of me on the flyleaf of my most recent book. My eyes had the appearance of being half-closed in an inscrutable, benevolent sort of a way, my rounded cheeks pushed up against my eyes, my lips were thick and smiling. I had become the Buddha. (Or 'the Blob' as I called myself later, thinking of the slow-moving redcurrant jelly that eats people in the movie starring Steve McQueen. I need jokey images like that to keep me going.)

Was I about to go on a course of treatment which would end up with me looking like the woman on the right? She looked a bit like Vera Lynn, so I thought that would be a remarkable transformation indeed.

I processed these thoughts in just a few seconds and after I had, I was overwhelmed with a deep sadness. My list of seemingly disconnected symptoms collapsed into one case: me. I saw 12 or more years of my life as lost to a disease, so much wasted time, stretching all the way back to me aged 19, looking at the puffiness on the back of my hand. I was quite literally feeling sorry for myself, sorry for the person that is me. I used to be zippy, energetic, quick-witted and I had just let it go, explained it away, and lost the old me without a complaint. Why hadn't I fought to save myself? What things might I have done in those lost years? I thought back to me being sacked from the BBC in 1972. Why had I just gone on the dole and waited for something to turn up? Why, when I had gone to film school in 1973, had I mostly drifted through, complaining that going on location was too cold for me?

And I had been in and out of relationships too. At the time, I had thought that I made decisions in the way that all of us make decisions: with our logical minds, of course. But was it possible my decisions had been shaped by how my thyroid controlled me? The things that I had done, not done and regretted . . . were they down to me being the Blob for all that time? In other words, was the life I was living right at that moment created by being the Blob? Never mind the lost years, I felt lost right there and then, overwhelmed by this chain of thoughts.

Mr Baker was on his feet.

'This is very exciting,' he said. 'I've got some students next door. I'll get them in to see if they can diagnose you. Don't tell them, OK?'

I nodded. He dashed out and brought back half a dozen young students. 'What's he got?' Mr Baker said to them. 'I'm going to leave the room and come back in again in two minutes' time.'

He left.

'What have you got?' one of the students said in my ear.

'I can't say,' I said, in a voice that I now know from old recordings that I've listened to was deep, coarse, and very, very slow, with the 's's slurred into 'sh's.

'I . . . can't . . . shay . . .'

The students looked at me, looked at each other and waited.

Mr Baker came back in. 'Well?' he said in his keen, bright way.

'Kidneys, sir,' one of them said.

'NO!' Mr Baker exploded. 'Just because we're in Renal, doesn't mean that he must therefore have problems with his kidneys! Have you taken his pulse? Have you touched his skin? Have you tested his reflexes? Have you asked him to walk across the room?'

At this he whipped out a little hammer and whacked my knee. My leg didn't budge.

'See that!' Mr Baker was shouting now. 'Nothing! No response at all. Feel his skin!' He put his fingertips on my cheek and neck. 'Clammy! Cold and clammy!' he shouted. 'Now, Mr Rosen, walk across the room, putting one foot directly in front of the other foot, heel of the front foot touching the toes of the rear foot.'

I tried. I couldn't.

'See that!' Mr Baker said. 'He's 35 and he can't even walk toe-to-heel across the floor! Look at the puffiness round his eyes! And his hands!'

He grabbed my wrist and felt the pulse for just a few seconds.

'It's way below what you'd expect. OK, what's he got?'

They didn't know.

'He's hypothyroid!' Mr Baker explained. 'It's very unusual. He's male and young. It's Hashimoto's: an autoimmune disease. Remember? His antibodies have identified his thyroid as a foreign body and digested it.'

He ushered the students out. Since then, I've often thought that somewhere out there in hospitals there must be half a dozen doctors – now in their sixties – who remember their lesson in hypothyroidism, coming face to face with sluggish, old me.

Mr Baker told me that to check if his diagnosis was correct, he would order a blood test and that I should come back to the Metabolic Unit in two weeks' time.

This was before the age of the internet, but I still had my old medical textbook and spent a good deal of time over the next two weeks reading about the symptoms of hypothyroidism and staring at the plumped-up version of Vera Lynn. I cursed myself over and over again for not having used one of the few bits of medical knowledge I had in my head to self-diagnose hypothyroidism. Those pieces of junk-shop furniture had been of no use. I felt stupid, and sorry that I had not been able to look after myself. These are not great feelings to have about yourself.

A fortnight later, I arrived at the Metabolic Unit, not knowing what such a word meant. I was met by Dr Gesundheit. In German, the word means 'health', and in all the times since 1981 that I've told people Dr Gesundheit's name, I haven't met anyone who believes me. They're sure that it's something I've added to the story as a gag. All I can say is that if you google Dr Gesundheit and 'endocrinology' you will find him with colleagues, with students and patients at Stanford University. Well, he was definitely there last time I looked.

Dr Gesundheit had my notes. He read them, looked at me and said in his American accent, 'Technically, you're dead. Or if not dead, you should be in a torpor.' He went on. 'Your antibodies have consumed your thyroid gland and now there aren't even any of those antibodies left. I don't know how it is that you're still standing.'

I thought of Weebles. *Weebles wobble, but they don't fall down.* I tried to tell Dr Gesundheit that I had been out with some teenagers on the Isle of Dogs, writing poems about dead dogsh, but of course it didn't come out very clearly. Anyway, he had an urgent matter to deal with: me.

'You have to come in straight away,' he said. 'I really can't risk you walking about anymore.'

I explained that I didn't have any shtuff with me and that I would have to go home firsht. He gave me permission to go home and come back in the next day.

I did just that.

I was given a bed in the ward in the metabolic unit, but first I went to sit in the communal area. I met a woman who was completely round, twice over. She had a round body, no neck and a round bald head. She explained to me that her glands weren't working. And there was a staggeringly tall man, with a long giant's face, great long ears, huge hands and feet and a roaring voice. When he talked, he barked. He said he had acromegaly, a rare condition where the body produces too much growth hormone. I was going to share a room with a boy aged about 15 and he was tiny – about the size of six-year-old. He told me that he had no growth hormone. 'What have you got?' they asked me.

'I'm hypothyroid,' I said.

'Yes,' said the woman who I was calling 'Ball Lady' (privately, to myself), 'you look weird.'

The others agreed. The giant, the tiny boy and one or two more, they all reckoned I looked weird.

'What happensh here?' I asked.

'We wait for the treatment to work,' roared the giant.

Ball Lady looked sad.

'They haven't found anything that works for me,' she said. 'I hope it works out for you.'

So I spent two weeks in the metabolic ward, not feeling even the tiniest bit ill. Quite the contrary. You see, each day, they brought me a little pile of white powder on a sheet of paper. I had to lick it off. After a few days, I felt stronger and lighter. When I looked in the mirror, I started to see the puffiness of my eyelids shrink. I caught sight of at least one knuckle on my hand. I had a sense of being able to see and think more clearly.

It felt like magic. A 12-year-long illness was being cured. The wonders of modern medicine.

And that's it. Every day since March 1981, I take thyroxine pills to stop me turning back into the Blob.

That's the end of the story.

But it isn't.

This body, that first had a thyroid gland, then consumed it, and then started using a substitute instead, has a mind attached. It's a mind that both listens to and talks to the body. This mind has tried to relate to at least three versions of the body: Pre-Blob, the Blob and Post-Blob. As you might imagine, the Post-Blob version started out in 1981, having huge problems with the other two versions. And pretty soon I was struggling with who I had become in the aftermath. In short, who was I? Who is the essence of me? Had I picked up where I left off, 12 years earlier? Could I just pretend that those 12 years hadn't happened? And something else had changed: that person in the last few months of the 12 years had become very slow, very unreactive, very passive. This Post-Blob one was loud, speedy, short-tempered, highly reactive and excitable.

Not that I knew it at the time, but I was someone now in desperate need of help and advice. I needed to have a space to talk about what had happened, and what I had gone through. I had got better physically, but I wasn't better 'in myself'. All around, people were happy for me. They were congratulating me on how well I looked. Some thought that I had made great efforts – finally! – to get fit. I went along with them because on one level, I really was pleased. I was 'saved'. Thinking of what Dr Gesundheit said, I thought it was a near-miss. A few more days and I might have gone into his 'torpor' (I always hear that in his American accent).

Behind my happy face, I started doing some strange things as I tried to knit my three selves together. When we have huge disruptions to our lives, like a serious illness or chronic condition, I think we have an impulse to try to bring all the different parts of ourselves in under one roof. No matter how divergent those parts were, I was sure that I was still one person, if only I could get the different bits to align. When I sat thinking about how separate the different parts were, it became unbearable. It defied understanding. Trying to pull myself together was a longing for coherence, connections, explanations, sense, in a situation when it wasn't always possible to find those things.

In the first months – years, possibly – I didn't and couldn't do the knitting. I just pretended I could.

I hid my distress. I hid it by doing several different things at the same time: apologies, reinvention and, as you'll read later, going running.

Apologies: I had a strong feeling that I needed to

go and apologise to people who I had behaved wrongly towards because of the Blob. At first, I went to see some people. So I said sorry, and then I said that I thought it was the Blob's fault. That didn't go down well. They said that I would have behaved like that anyway. I think people spotted that I was trying to explain my behaviour and my personality as if it was all created by one hormone. Simple explanations like this can be comforting. But I also came face to face with people who spotted that I wasn't really saying sorry. I was both explaining away how I had been with one simple reason, and using that simple reason as a way to be forgiven. I saw that people didn't like it. I could see that they were right not to like it! So I dropped the Blob alibi.

The second route that I took was reinvention. Now that I was a 'new man', I started doing new things. That makes it sound as if I did this in a logical, thought-out way. I can see now that some of the things I did were just the opposite: I did some things on impulse, throwing away things that made me secure and safe. I know why now: I gave myself a bit of a superman complex. After all, at my Dr Gesundheit moment, I was on the verge of collapse. Every part of my body was lacking in the hormone that enables us to turn food into energy. Now, I was virtually back to where I had been when I was 19 or 20. Nagging away at the back of my mind, though, was that I had lost my twenties. It was absurd that I felt as extremely as that because I had done a lot of things in that time – written books, made recordings, done hundreds of school visits, worked in schools as a writing teacher, written articles, made schools' TV programmes . . . and so on. But I diminished it and kept thinking of it as 'lost time'.

Some of the impulse stuff was fine, especially at work. I helped create two children's TV series, *Everybody Here* and *Black and White and Read All Over*, and created a character, Dr Smartypants, who I was proud of and thought at the time had legs for more series. But on the personal front, it was pretty disastrous. Don't ask why. Just take it that it was. And it goes without saying that I really don't know whether what I did was a result of the chemical turbulence of the moment, the whole cycle of going into hypothyroidism and then coming out of it, my personality, or a combination of all three.

If I look at this through the prism of 'getting better', all I can say is that I definitely 'got better' physically – that's what the pills do. In the end though, it feels as if the mental whirlwind has only really settled down with the passing of time. The distress has disappeared under the sand of new things. And that's OK. The old cliché 'time's a great healer' makes sense to me. It didn't work in the past. At my age, it does.

Chapter 4

We think it would be better if you went freelance

Two big things happened in my life while I was grappling with my illness. Looking at them now, they are both examples of how I was in the grip of passivity. For years, I've wondered whether this was a direct result of not having enough thyroid hormones in my body, or whether that lack exaggerated something that was already in my personality. And I suppose there's another possibility too: that it's got nothing to do with the thyroid. These are the tangled webs that people who have severe illnesses can get into, and I want to explore them more here.

Now for the two things.

The first: I was sacked. The second: my mother died.

These happened around the midpoint of my downward spiral to becoming the Blob, and I reacted to them strangely. Of course, the problem was that I didn't know at the time why I was behaving in these strange ways.

First, let me tell you about the job. I was what was called a General Trainee at the BBC. Though this sounds like I was being trained to be a handyman, in fact it was regarded within the BBC as highly prestigious training in radio, TV and film production. The traineeships were handed out to only six people a year and the training route I followed took me through radio drama and drama documentaries, BBC television's programme for under-fives, *Play School*, and then on to Schools TV – perfect for a children's writer like me. I did indeed learn how to make and direct radio and TV programmes and films. You can try to picture me now, poring over scripts, sitting in radio and TV 'galleries' with producers directing the actors, designers, recording engineers and so on. At times, I was allowed to take the lead and direct too. I had a bit of knowledge. I had spent five years or so doing drama classes at the Questors Theatre in Ealing and had written, acted in or directed many plays at university. I had also written a play that had been put on at the Royal Court Theatre in London. The BBC work all felt like familiar territory, but remember – all the while, I'm gradually slowing down, swelling up, going white, feeling cold and talking with slurred speech.

I remember (with embarrassment) one time I was sitting in the gallery directing *Play School*. Above my head in front of me is a row of monitors showing what each of the cameras is filming, plus one more, which is the 'output' monitor – that is the view that people at home will see. Sitting next to me is the vision mixer, who does what I ask them to do. So when I say, 'Coming to camera three . . . and go!' or some such, the vision mixer presses buttons and we see what camera three sees. Meanwhile, I am also telling each camera person to get ready for the next shot by moving in closer, or further away, or remembering to 'pan' left or right, or to 'tilt' up and down. It's all pretty complicated because you're delivering instructions to five, six or more people if changes of lighting and sound are involved too. (This, at least, was how it worked nearly 50 years ago!) Down below us in the studio are two presenters, let's say it was Johnny Ball and Julie Stevens. With them are Big Ted, Little Ted, Jemima and Hamble. Over there is the Round Window, the Arched Window and the Square Window. As it's a TV studio, everything down there is super-bright and colourful – rather like the back of a cereal packet.

As I am a trainee, there are various people watching over me to see how I'm doing, one of whom is sitting right next to me, to cover for me if I forget something. This is all pretty tense, because you only have a limited time to get it right. And don't forget it's my job to make sure the presenters get their words right, stick to the script that I've written and do what we agreed in rehearsal. There's very little room for error, because you know you can't come back tomorrow and do it all again. Even though it's a recording rather than a live broadcast, there is only a very limited time allotted to film what is required. No overruns, no second chances.

On this particular day, we're all ready to go when the senior producer (who is sitting next to me) says that she would like to introduce something new to the show. She has come up with the idea that we should have a magnetic board with figures on it. These figures are people in jobs, like a nurse or a footballer. They are wearing their work clothes and on the board there are more clothes that match each of the figures, like a football shirt for the footballer, and a nurse's apron for the nurse. The producer says she wants the presenters to play a game of trying to match the clothes up, like it's as hard as it would be for the three-year-old watching at home. They're supposed to improvise things, and I haven't scripted this, which means that I haven't worked out the camera shots. In other words, I haven't worked out which camera should show the whole scene (called 'the wide' in TV language) nor which one should take the close-up of the magnet board. I'm beginning to get panicky. Well, as panicky as the Blob can feel. Everything starts to spin. I can't think of what to say to the vision mixer.

The senior producer then says something which was obvious to her, like, 'Oh, grab the close-ups on Three, take the singles on One and Four, and Two can take the wide.' I freeze. All my preparation has gone down the pan and in that instant, I decide something about myself: I can't be the kind of spontaneous, slick sort of a guy who can do what she is asking me to do. In a single moment, my confidence disappears. Years later, I wonder whether if I hadn't been hypo-thyroid, I might have been able to do it, but this slow, furred-up version of myself just couldn't handle it. What I did next is an absolute no-no in the world of TV. I stood up, looked at the senior producer and said, 'I can't do it. You do it.' Shock horror: I had left the chair! No director leaves the chair. But I did. To this day, I blush to think about it.

Of course, now I've got an excuse: my illness. But at the time, I had no way out. I was face to face with my own uselessness. It might seem like a minor moment, but for me it felt monumental, a sign of my own failure, and we all have moments like that – the seemingly small incidents that we remember as a sign of our weaknesses. Even today, there's a nagging doubt about myself that maybe I'd have failed any-way, without being ill. Then and there, I defined myself as a guy who simply is not up to it. Accepting this, at the time, was a coping strategy. It wasn't a nice thing to do, especially as I marvelled at the way the full-time directors directed their programmes, calling the shots, marshalling the whole thing as if they were maestros conducting a symphony orchestra. I felt inadequate by comparison.

Soon, I went to work for Schools TV, but the experience continued to affect me. At Schools TV, I found myself scripting a teaching-to-read series for very young children. I called it *Sam on Boffs' Island*. I devised a 20-part series where dreamy Sam had a real life in the everyday world, but dreams himself away to the island of the Boffs. These were puppet humans made by Peter Firmin and directed by the great Oliver Postgate, famous by then for the Clangers, Noggin the Nog and Ivor the Engine. The BBC loved my idea and I wrote ten of the scripts. I helped with the casting and we chose Tony Robinson as Sam, with his mum played by Miriam Margolyes (yes, really!). I introduced an idea that was something new to teaching-to-read TV programmes on the BBC: songs that the Boffs would sing and would be learned by the children to help them read. At the time, I was working with Ewan MacColl, and two people in the group were John Faulkner and Sandra Kerr (who went on to sing all the songs, and play all the parts, in Oliver Postgate's great show *Bagpuss* – perhaps in spite of my failures I was midwife for a great creative partnership!). I wrote the lyrics and John and Sandra wrote the music and sang them in a folk style.

The producer of *Sam on Boffs' Island* asked me to come out on location to shoot Tony and Miriam doing the 'realistic' bits, then to come and see Oliver and Peter to watch them build the puppets, and to come on to the Ealing Film Studios 'stage' (where they had shot the Ealing Comedies) to film the bits where the Boffs are in a boat. She constantly asked me if I wanted to direct some of the programmes myself and I kept saying no. I doubted myself. I felt I couldn't do it. It distresses me to think this now. It was a fantastic opportunity to complete the full menu of programme-making: coming up with an idea, scripting it, auditioning actors, directing them and shooting them on location or in studio and then editing it all in post-production. In truth, I would have loved to do it: it is one of my big regrets that I didn't. Instead, feeling the fear, I turned it down. I feel in myself that if I had been well, I would have grabbed that chance and that I might well have gone on to work in children's TV as a mixture of scriptwriter, director and perhaps as a presenter or performer too. This was my moment and I blew it. In my mind, I replay the moment again and again: I can see the producer saying to me, 'OK, Michael, would you like to direct this next sequence?' And I'm saying, 'No, thanks.' I think all of us have these moments, when our beliefs about ourselves stop us doing the things we really want to do.

It's hard for me to accept this, even now. Sometimes, in my mind, I demand of the people I knew well or lived with, *why didn't you notice I was ill? Why didn't you tell me what I looked and sounded like? Wasn't it obvious?* And no reply comes. What do I do with this thought, though? How do I cope with it? In that moment when Mr Baker said, 'You're hypothyroid', this time at the BBC was one of the scenes that flashed through my mind. I saw myself ducking out of directing the TV programme, and felt a wave of regret.

So, how do we deal with this? Now – a bit less than 50 years later – I can compensate for this regret and feeling of lost time by weighing it up against what I've done, starting out from the time I started getting better. I play a balancing game. 'I may have missed out with *Sam on Boffs' Island*, but haven't my son and I created a YouTube channel of my poetry that has had over a 100 million views?' That works. 'Balancing', as I've called it, is what makes loss and failure (and the regret about loss and failure) bearable. I'm very aware that not everyone can do it. I realise that I am very lucky, to be someone who has done the kind of stuff that lets them think in this way. And anyway, what can you do with regret? I'm sounding like my mother now, aren't I? Regret is alright as far as it goes, but you can't ever do anything with it. It just sits on your head like a cold, wet flannel, slowing you down.

Back to *Sam on Boffs' Island*, though, where I was still struggling: I found that I couldn't write any more than ten programmes. I got writer's block, so the producer said she would hire someone to write the other ten. I overheard her negotiating his fee. In my slow mind, I figured out that something wasn't quite right: I had created a new TV series and I was only getting my BBC traineeship salary to do it. I raised the matter with the producer and I was slapped down pretty sharpish. What she told me was that this is how the BBC works. If you're a producer and you script a programme, that's part of your job. I tried to say that I had gone beyond that, because I had devised a whole series. No, she explained, that's what it's like here. Next point, she said, you're a trainee. Consider yourself lucky that you've been given this chance. It's part of your training. That was me told!

The BBC had made very clear that there was no promise of a job at the end of the two and a half years of training, but that we were very well placed to apply for jobs. I did. And in the informal way that big organisations sometimes operate, I heard on the grapevine that I was successful with one of these. Then a few days later, I heard that I wasn't.

Soon, I found that my 'attachments' to different

departments across the whole BBC also dried up. Instead of being posted to the World Service or to Light Entertainment or some such, as was usually the case, there was nothing for me. Even stranger, I heard – again on the grapevine – that there was a department that wanted me to come and join them. But – weirdly – it was decided from on high that I wasn't allowed to go. So I sat at home, on full pay, waiting to be called. I just lolled about, doing nothing. All day.

It was demoralising. In the space of less than three years I had dropped from directing TV programmes for BBC 2 and devising a whole Schools TV series to getting up at midday to sit at home and do nothing. Meanwhile, I knew that my old friend Nigel Williams was having a great time working in Arts Features. I wonder now if my hesitations and my own lack of confidence had been picked up on.

How did I cope? I tried shrugging it off, of course! In a way, the passivity caused by my underactive thyroid gland helped. The passivity powered the shrug. Shrugging off humiliation is quite a skill to acquire. If I learned anything from this time, it's how to shrug. I am an expert shrugger.

After about three months of sitting all day in my flat, I got a call. I had to come in to meet Head of Staff Training (known as 'HST') to discuss my future at the big grey BBC building near Oxford Circus, sometimes called the 'Battleship'. I walked slowly through the great heavy brown art deco doors, going up in the old brown art deco lifts into one of the rooms that overlooks the street that runs towards Oxford Circus tube station. I was met by HST, a tall, upright man who had been in the navy. I think he may have been an admiral. He was very friendly and immediately started to tell me how talented I was. I thought this was odd, because the experience of the last three months seemed to be all about me being not talented. He told me that it was most impressive that I had come up with this teaching-to-read series for Schools TV. In fact, he said, he had a proposal: I was so talented that he thought it would be better if I went freelance.

Freelance? I thought. *Wow, that sounds great. It's a kind of promotion, isn't it?* I've done so well, here's HST himself thinking that I can now sell programmes to the BBC from outside and that way, I won't get to feel that somehow or other I've been cheated. What's more, HST added, the BBC can offer you an ex gratia payment of £400.

I couldn't believe it. Success!

I walked out the door, back down in the lift, out through those heavy doors and down the street. It took me the time it takes to get from Broadcasting House to Oxford Circus Station to realise that I had been sacked. I was now out of a job. Unemployed. I had no work. I had fallen for HST's schmooze about me being talented and how great it would be if I went freelance whereas in actual fact it was nothing more or less than being given the boot. It became clearer and clearer to me that I had failed.

Even in my current state of health, I did start to figure out that I had to get on and do something. In some ways, perhaps the sacking gave me the impetus to put myself out there again. I was writing poems and stories and there was one corner of the BBC that was still employing me, Schools Radio. I also met up with someone who was at the time a friend of a friend: Nick Broomfield, now of great film-making fame. He was a first-year student at what was then the National Film School, he encouraged me to apply and I got in. I even got a grant from my local council for me to study there for three years.

All of this fits into a well-known formula: if you're stuck in a hole, thinking that you're a failure or that you've been rejected, the best thing you can do is to pull yourself up, to be active. Of course, that is nothing more than words if you don't have access to the resources or the opportunities – certainly, grants are much harder to come by these days, and we don't all 'know someone'. We don't all start from the same spot or carry the same baggage – good or bad. But the principle of activity, of getting going, is still important. Find something you enjoy, and go for it. Activity helped me. The poems I wrote for the Schools Radio programme turned into my first book for children. The book led me into performing in schools, libraries and theatres – a job I've done and loved ever since.

Film school was another matter. In a way, it took me down the same dead end I reached at the BBC: realising that I didn't have the energy or the where-withal to make films as I watched my talented peers grab their cameras and sound gear, going out, shoot-ing films and sitting for hours and hours in editing suites putting them together. Even more amazing – don't laugh – they didn't appear to freeze to death doing it. It seemed to me that being on location in winter in England was like being at the North Pole. Sitting in poorly heated editing suites – which at that time at the film school were little more than Ministry of Defence prefab huts – felt like being in a prison cell.

I was going downhill again, not grabbing the opportunities that were sitting there on a plate in front of me. I started to become detached from the place, spending more time at home than at the cam-pus. I couldn't drum up the effort to get myself from north London all the way to Beaconsfield in Bucking-hamshire. I was increasingly apologising for myself for being not able to do things. Now, I see that it was more passivity.

Then my mother died.

She had spotted a small lump under her tongue. She was 54, living only a couple of miles away from me as I was going (or not going) to film school. Over two years, Mum went from working as an education lecturer to being an invalid at home with a cancer that spread from her jaw to her lungs. It was a horrifying decline from running university courses, doing talks and workshops for hundreds of teachers and writing articles to being incapacitated. Worse, she had an operation that took away half her jaw. She hated what she looked like and hid herself in the bedroom, seeing only one or two people. It was a grim, heartless time, with no comfort. I thought that there was some hope she'd be all right and I think my father and brother did too, but in reality there wasn't. She had some chemotherapy but I remember her wailing that she couldn't bear the headaches anymore and stopped it.

For a while, I moved back home and lived with my parents, as I thought it would help the situation. It didn't. I fear I didn't do enough of the fetching, carrying and cleaning that would have taken the burden from my father. More thyroid effects, I suspect. He was suffering. He had been with my mother since they were both 17. They had both a family and work relationship – they were starting to write articles and books together as their interests in children's language developed. Both relationships – their lives – were on the verge of being shattered. I can remember my father walking out of the room on one occasion, crying helplessly. Another time, even more awfully, a surgeon told us some test results had come back. 'It's positive,' he said. My father clapped his hands together, 'Thank goodness!' he said. 'No,' said the surgeon, 'what I mean is that the results show that the cancer is still there.' The word 'positive' meant one thing to the surgeon and the opposite to my father. What a terrible irony for someone who had spent his whole life immersed in the meaning and use of words.

I saw my mother die. We were in the bedroom, and my father had a nurse coming to the house. I think I still reckoned that at some point, Mum would win through, battered and wrecked though she was. She sat up in bed, coughed, spluttered, some matter came out of her mouth and she flopped back. The nurse – an Irish woman – moved swiftly and calmly forwards, wiped Mum's face, laid her gently back on to the pillow and told us she was dead. My father rocked to and fro next to the bed.

You may have noticed that I'm talking here mostly as a witness, outside of the action. I'm not really saying much about what I thought or how I thought. This disturbs me. To tell the truth – and it shocks me – I felt numb. One reason for this might have been that my hypothyroidism was so advanced that I had started to lose the ability to feel emotions in any deep or affecting way. It was as if the swollen tissues, the puffiness, had started to affect my brain. I know this isn't fully true and yet that's how it feels to me, looking back. I keep asking myself, why didn't I care in the way my father and brother clearly did? They were hurting. I was there but not there. I wasn't full of dread that I might be losing one of the most important people in my life.

In the now, I have to find a way of handling this. After all, when tragic or sad things have happened in my life since I came out of that hypothyroid bubble, I've been as raw and upset as anyone. I have to ask myself, was the cause of my numbness really, really, really the lack of thyroxine in my bloodstream or was it some kind of repressed attitude to my mother? It's a horrific question to ask myself: is there some part of me that, deep down, was actually indifferent to her dying? Then again, perhaps it was my way of dealing with the shock, a kind of defence mechanism. Can I (should I?) really put it all down to my bloody thyroid gland?

In a way, these are unanswerable questions, but that's the point – when you struggle with illness, it's hard to see where 'it' stops and you begin. I know that many, many times since my mother died, I've wanted her to be there to talk to, to listen to. I've desperately wanted her to be part of my children's lives but she died when my oldest was still in the womb. She left. He arrived.

My father and I went to see Mum at the under-taker's. We stood next to her, side by side. He then put his hands up to his face, making them into two book-ends by his temples. He moved his hands towards Mum and back, saying something under his breath about remembering her face. Her poor face, mutilated by the operation, her nose shrunk down to nothing more than a beak, her skin shiny and grey. I thought that this must be the worst thing that had ever happened to him.

I also think about the funeral. Hundreds of people were there. As I remember, my father planned it on his own. Whether because it's what he wanted to do or because I thought it's what he wanted to do, I took a step back. On the day, I remember feeling apart. The funeral didn't feel like anything to do with Mum. Some of the speeches came from people I hardly knew or who hadn't come to see her as she was dying. I felt cross. I remember sitting down outside after-wards and people walking past me saying how sorry they were. Plenty of people cried. I didn't.

I feel guilty and odd about this. It's difficult for me to admit to. It annoys me to tell myself that I was like that.

All I can 'do' with it now, I figure, is to accept that's how I was. I can't like it, but it's best for me to not hate it. I can tell myself that, for whatever reasons, I have never experienced that kind of numbness since that moment of revelation with Mr Baker in the renal unit in 1981. This helps me. You can tell me, if you like, that I've simply found an alibi. I've told myself as much on occasions. I can blame the activity – or inactivity rather – of my thyroid gland, and as weird as that sounds, it is some kind of help. Of course, in another way – if I tell myself of all the missed opportunities of those years – it's not much help at all.

My father chose not to make any memorial for my mother. There is no stone, plaque or inscription anywhere. I don't know for certain why this is. One reason may be that it's part of my mother's outlook: after all, there were no pictures in our home, no grave for Alan, the brother who died, so maybe Mum told Dad that it should be the same for her. She was always moving on.

One postscript: in 1984, some 11 years after I was sacked from the BBC, and three years after my moment with Mr Baker, a man knocked on my door to talk about what had happened with the BBC. 'Why do you think you were sacked?' he asked me. I said, in a flippant way, 'I couldn't get up in the morning. I had an underactive thyroid.' 'No,' he said, 'MI5 didn't want you to have a full-time job at the BBC. You were deemed to be too left wing.' He went on to to tell me an elaborate story about BBC committees, special files marked by Christmas trees (I kid you not), an office in that very same 'battleship' building just down the corridor from HST and five other BBC employees similarly dealt with. What's more, he said, they were going to print the story in the *Observer* in a few days' time.

What?! I was bowled over. On one level, it seemed like something out of a movie. On another, if what he was saying was true, it was creepy. I thought of that series of meetings I had had with people in charge of general trainees, assuring me with regret in their voices that they were doing what they could to make sure that I got a job, that departments couldn't have me as an 'attachment' for complicated financial reasons. They had always been so kind and so sorry. I remembered dark offices full of old green filing cabinets, lino floors and secretaries next door walking in and out with files. Did one of them have a Christmas tree on it?

At a deep level, I thought, isn't this how really bad stuff happens? People at the top make decisions about who is undesirable, and lower-down functionaries keep the undesirable person in the dark?

Sure enough, the article came out – a double spread in the *Observer*, my photo along with the others all lined up across the top. No one denied the truth of it. The journalists had got a scoop.

Where did it leave me, though? I still think that my thyroid let me down. Or rather, my failure to spot that my thyroid had failed let me down. I could have made a success of the traineeship. But I also think that I actually did OK as far as *Sam on Boffs' Island* goes. If I had been more together, I might have been even more likely to have got the chop, an even more unwanted figure. On that row of mugshots in the *Observer* there were some talented and successful people who had been deemed to be a threat precisely because they were active and doing good work.

It all makes me think that when a crisis happens in your life, there are nearly always different angles on it. Like a lot of things in my life, I've found a way to package it up so that it doesn't hurt, it doesn't incapacitate me, it doesn't prevent me from carrying on or being active. It's as if I can put it in a box, put the box in the cupboard and shut the door on it. If I want to take it out – as I've done here – I can do it without that awful look of regret that I saw on my father's face all those years ago. But even so, that business of putting it in a box, even one in my head, is a bit like my father's cousin, isn't it? Putting the box of photos of the relatives who died in the Holocaust into a cupboard and locking the door. Or perhaps it's like my father not making a place with Mum's name on it.

*

But as you know, eventually I got better. And, in contrast to the passivity I had felt, it was when I started moving, quite literally, that I felt myself again. One of the first things I did after my medication helped to improve my health was to take up running. It was a miracle. The first place I ran was Hackney Marshes, the very place where I had thought there were hills. I ran and ran and ran. I bought running magazines. I bought trainers. I timed myself. I drew charts and listed my personal bests. The moment I met someone who was a runner, I'd get into intense conversations about ankles or training by running backwards.

This was all thrilling. I felt like a living example of the cliché: I was a new man. Here was hard evidence that I was no longer the Blob. Looking back on myself at that moment, part of me wants to mock my new obsession, but another part of me wants to celebrate it. There is something hypnotic and exhilarating about running. There's the rhythm of your legs and arms. There's a sense of power that comes from the feeling that you can move over pavements, parks and hills faster than our usual everyday way of doing it. If you do a lot of it, it starts to affect how you are in the rest of your day: the way you walk upstairs, the way you sit, how your legs feel, how you eat and how you breathe. It's that total. From being the Blob to being able to run and run and run was a thrill.

I started to do fun runs and charity runs. I ran a half-marathon. I even wanted to run in the London Marathon. And, of course, I used to sit and talk about how I liked running to people who didn't run. I guess I graduated to being a fully qualified running bore. One day I was proving that I was just that: I was telling someone about where I had run to that day and how I was wondering if I could make it even further next time. And they said, 'If I were you, I would worry less about where you're running to and think about what you're running from.'

Now that pulled me up sharp. What did they mean? What insight lay in that provocative little thought?

Chapter 5

It doesn't go like that, does it, boys and girls?

This chapter is about school, education, learning and studying – right through our lives. I was at school myself once, of course, but from my thirties onwards I've worked a lot in schools alongside teachers, helping children write. For over three decades I've also taught teachers about children's reading and writing in schools and universities. And, as you'll see, I've also spent time adding on some education for myself as an adult. In all this time, whether on the receiving or giving end of education, I've been interested in what encourages us, and the opposite – what discourages us, both of which happen often in the classroom.

We walk around with voices in our heads: the voices of the people who've encouraged us, slapped us down, pumped us up, mocked us, admired us . . .

If we line them up in front of us, they're like the ups and downs in a cycle race, one moment sending us flying on our way, the next leaving us struggling to keep going. In ancient myths like *The Odyssey* or in big Victorian novels like *Great Expectations*, the hero has to deal with people who help them and with other people who hinder them. I've noticed that we can easily be pulled down or dragged back by a persistent negative voice in our heads. Let me say in passing, I'm not referring here to cases of abuse. I'm not qualified to talk of these. But where I do have some experience is in the field of discouragement: those off-putting hints, comments and put-downs that can live with us – haunt us even – through our whole lives. Meanwhile, if we dig around in our minds, we can also find people who liked something that we had done – saw something special in us, even – and said so. These forms of praise are also a big deal.

We have these voices in our heads that compete: negative versus positive, knocking down versus building up, affirming versus undermining. The trick, then, is to handle these so that we can walk a path that is neither so low that we can't go forwards, nor so high that we end up thinking we're better than everyone else. The way we encounter positive and negative voices in education is an experience that shapes us all.

In the best of all possible worlds, the simple fact of mentioning education would give anyone a warm glow. School, or learning, would make us think of our minds expanding, gaining new insights, moments full of discovery, exciting times when we felt ourselves creating something new. Then, as we think of these, we hear in our heads appreciative comments from friends, teachers, parents and family . . . OK, dream over, what's it really like?

I'll be positive first: do you have any moments from school or college that are at least a bit like that? I'll be honest – I do! If you do too, it's worth mulling them over, jotting them down even. They are gold dust. I can remember an English teacher asking me to read out what we used to call a 'composition' (a kind of story) to the rest of the class. She said, 'One day you'll be a writer.' It was probably a pain in the bum for the rest of the class to hear that, but I hang on to it all the same. I can see a PE teacher pushing me to 'go for it' in his strong Cornish accent in some circuit training in the gym. I can hear the wonderful old crusty voice of a tutor at university telling me I had said some really interesting things in an essay where I had compared two poems.

But then there's one of the most humiliating moments in my life: an oral exam where a row of university tutors quizzed me. At the university I attended, if your written exams led the examiners to think you were either going to fail or that you were on the edge of getting a 'first' (the top degree), you were invited to a cross-examination by 12 examiners, all dressed up in their suits, white ties and gowns, in an ornate eighteenth-century room. I was borderline 'first' but the chief examiner, clothed in her ceremonial crimson-coloured waistcoat, decided that I needed a dressing-down. Whereas all the other examiners had given me marks worth a first, the chief examiner had marked the one paper she was responsible for as a fail. She then proceeded to sneer at and mock what I had written, as if I was on trial. This was particularly odd, as the one question she appeared to be most angry about was based on a piece of original research I had done on plays that she had never heard of.

In fact, so convinced was she that I was a disreputable, unworthy creature, she had at first assumed that I had made up these plays! She had trogged off to the university library to read them – in her case, for the first time in her life. In this cross-examination (very cross, actually), she poured scorn and derision on someone who would be so stupid as to write about such little-known plays. As I say, it was a humiliating moment and felt more like I had failed the whole course rather than reached to the edge of getting a first. The sting of it has stayed with me, and we all have similar examples in our own lives.

But as I left – doing the long walk past the begowned examiners, one of the others, a very mild-mannered guy, leaned over and whispered to me that he thought that the exam paper he had marked was one of the best he had ever read. Here I was, being roasted in public, and he was supposed to be falling in behind the very famous chief examiner, in her crimson tabard. I've often thought that by whispering that to me he knew he was doing just about the most daredevil thing he had ever done. And it's a comfort that he did. If I want to feel lousy, I can think of the crimson tabard. If I want to feel better, I can see that chap leaning towards me, trying to be nice to me. It's amazing how you can run the same story through your head in different ways, transforming it from positive to negative.

I'm reminded of another story that has stuck with me: a new teacher arrived at my school when I was 17. He explained that he didn't understand the book we would be studying that year. We all looked at each other. What kind of teacher does that? What's the point of coming to school to learn stuff if the teacher themselves doesn't understand it? He said that we would read the book together and help each other to 'get it'. I went home and told my dad about this and he said, 'Very clever! That's an old dodge. He knows that book inside out. It's just a trick to get you lot to talk.' *Fair enough*, I thought.

Sure enough, we went through the book, line by line, 'helping' Mr Spearman with it. We chipped in, discussed possible meanings, argued about it and then wrote our essays. Many years later, I was at a teachers' meeting somewhere and there was Mr Spearman. He was a headteacher by then and he came over to me. We chatted for a bit about what he and I were up to and then he said, 'Do you remember that book I was supposed to be teaching you and your class that year?' 'Yes,' I said. 'You know, Michael,' he said, 'I had no idea what it was about but you and your classmates talked it through. I think it was one of the best years of teaching I ever did.'

I love that story. It reminds of a time when school gave me a sense of 'can-do'. And it didn't come to me because someone said, 'You can do it', but through the doing itself. Simply by actually doing it, we realised we *could* do it. And Mr Spearman's modesty and kindness was what gave us the confidence to give it a go. It was a special way to get better at doing something.

Of course, that's not the only way school can give you an uplift. I can think of another teacher who we felt was unbelievably clever. The opposite of Mr Spearman, if you like. He was kind, friendly and appreciative, while showing us things in what we were reading that we hadn't dreamed of ourselves. It was like watching someone scrape away layers of earth to reveal treasure. The fact that he wanted to do that for us made me want to try to do that too: another way to get better. Both of these kinds of 'uplift', found in good experiences of education, can transform us so that we take pleasure in 'getting better'.

In my adult life, I have one education memory that stands out more than any other. A man called Sean invited me to come to his school to read my poems to the children. He said that they loved my stuff and they were very excited to meet me. The school was in north-west London and I was very new to this business of just turning up and reading to children. I had only done a bit of it so far in libraries and 'children's book groups' – a group of children sitting round in a nice book corner while I talked quietly about writing and read a few poems. Quite different to a school. What did Sean have in mind? I wondered.

When I got there, he took me into his room and showed me some paintings that the pupils had done. He was full of awe and respect for the children and kept looking at me and asking me what I thought. I said I thought the paintings were great but was still wondering what he had in store for me. Then he said, 'Well, Michael, this is it. The children have been waiting for you . . . and here they are!' He then flung open the door, and straight away I realised that his office had two doors: the private one I had come through and the other, which opened out on to the school hall. I was now suddenly standing in front of 400 children. Sean shouted out, 'It's Michael Rosen!' And there was a great roar from the 400.

I instantly wanted to run away. I had never spoken to 400 children at once and I certainly had never tried to read poems to an audience that big. Sean led me to the centre of the hall, where I stood in front of the 400 and nodded. I was supposed to start. I opened my book at any old page and started to read. I held the book up in front of my face, trying to hide. I should also say that I was at least six years into my hypothyroidism at this stage, so I was slow and slurred too. I started to read one of the poems – a silly nonsense piece about a man called Old Ben Brown who played the ukulele with his trousers down. Think of me, mumbling my way through that from behind my book!

Now, London children will give a speaker about four seconds before they decide whether you're worth listening to or not. If it's a no, then a lot of other things suddenly become much more interesting, like the velcro on their shoes, their hair, the sound their fingernails make on the floor. They were at this stuff in a matter of seconds. *Bshht! Fssht! Queeecccch!* My mouth went dry. I glanced across at Sean. He was looking at me in horror. He had picked up from my poems that I was some kind of livewire, but here I was, muttering and stumbling and slurring in front of the whole school. It was a disaster.

He took control of the situation. 'No, no, no!' he shouted to the whole school hall. 'It doesn't go like that, does it, boys and girls?' And a great roar came back, 'NOOOOOOO!!!!' He grabbed the book out of my hand and then half-sung, half-chanted, half-danced the poem. The whole audience of children joined in and they even turned the last line into a jazzy little number with a silent beat before the last word.

I was staggered. Amazed. I did also feel a failure. I hadn't known how to entertain 400 children. I had never seen anything done the way Sean did it. On the way home, I thought about it: these little poems I had written could be . . . performed? I could make them into jazz numbers? Which I could act out?

It was a turning point. I used my feeling of failure to wise up, and learn what it was that Sean had done. From that moment, I changed what I did. As it happens, I had spent my teen years and my years at university going to acting classes, acting in plays, writing plays, even directing plays, but I had never made the connection between poems and performing in front of children! *Der!* as my own children would say. But now, thanks to Sean, I got it. He was the catalyst that brought together the different things I had done in my life so that I could make something new. And I've been doing it ever since: writing things to perform, performing things to write, developing voices, facial expressions, moves, jokes, audience participation routines, songs, mimes and so on. Each time I do it, the buzz it gives me comes from a feeling that I am always trying to get better at it, do it right for that audience, that group of children on that day in that particular place. It's a big 'getting better' moment – perhaps the biggest in my professional life. The low feeling I had when I realised my limitations was the trigger for me to learn how to do better.

This, like my other good experiences of education, gave me what is called 'agency'. We have agency when we feel that we can do things ourselves that have an effect. Agency means that you are the doer. That effect may be on ourselves or on others or, most likely, on both. To state the obvious, if we have a good effect on others, that has a good effect on ourselves. We feel better. The opposite – when we feel we have no agency, might be OK for a while, but if it goes on and on, it's demoralising. You feel you have no control, no worth. I've been there too.

So, let's spend a bit of time thinking about being demoralised!

Here's a scene: Victoria Station. I'm 16 and I'm coming back from France on my own. I've just spent the previous six weeks in a French children's summer camp. I was the only English kid there so I've spent all that time only hearing and speaking French. Waiting for me at the station are my father and brother. I get into the car (an old Ford), my father driving, me next to him, my brother in the back. The conversation goes like this:

'You're not very brown,' my father says. 'I expected you would be really tanned.'

'Mmm,' I say, slightly disappointed. I had desperately wanted to look like the French kids, as I have a secret plan to become French.

'Your letters were pretty poor to start off with, but they got better,' he says.

'Mmm,' I say, wondering what is it about him that makes even letter-writing something to be commented on and marked?

We pull out of the station and head home.

'Aren't you going to ask about your exam results?'

'Oh yes, right, yeah,' I say. 'How did I get on?'

There's a pause.

'Not one A,' he says.

At this, my brother pipes up. 'Not one A!' he says, imitating the way my father has spoken. He says it again: 'Not one A!'

My father then ran through the marks, making the extra point that even the paper he had taught me, English Literature, wasn't an A either. My brother, meanwhile, is still chanting, 'Not one A' in the back and waving his hands about, miming and exaggerating our father's gestures.

What do I make of this scene and why do I remember it so clearly? One reason is that I felt bad. I felt that I was not good enough. I had disappointed my father, who I loved and admired enormously. This feeling, one of demoralisation, would be all that I would take from that scene if it wasn't for some 'work' that I've done on it.

As with all our family 'scenes', or any of these memories that endure, the backstories are what helps us make sense of them. If you have scenes in your head that keep coming back to you, even seem like they burn in your mind, then you might want to fill in the backstory. I offer it as a strategy that you can use to feel better, to regain agency when you think you might be stuck.

My Victoria Station moment is in a way more about my brother than me, so to get to its root we have to go back to my brother's time at school. At the time of the Victoria scene he was 20, but back when he was at school, he was deemed to be so clever that he skipped a whole year. He was bumped up from the first year at secondary school (now called Year 7) into the third year (now called Year 9). Even though he missed out a whole year, by the time he was doing the big exams in what is now Year 11 (Fifth Year, then) he had caught up with, and even exceeded, many of his peers, and was getting As. For some mysterious reason, though, this wasn't good enough for my dad. I can remember fraught scenes of our father complaining bitterly that my brother wasn't working hard enough, wasn't reading enough, was spending too much time on fiddling with his bike or throwing the javelin, or staying up to listen to radio commentaries of the Le Mans 24-hour motor race, or – work of the devil – making model cars! So there was a double hammer coming down on my brother – the you're-wasting-time one, and the your-marks-aren't-good-enough one.

This was all pretty tense, but my brother had a way of letting off steam about it. He was a brilliant mimic. When he and I were on our own, he would do perfect imitations of our father in full flow, complete with all his gestures. 'What's he doing up there? Spending bloody hours and hours painting the head-lights on a bloody plastic car!' I think – and I hope – that this helped my brother. Without being too dramatic about it, I hope that it dealt with his demons. Something else happened though: he became my lightning conductor. When my father started up similar complaints about my own work ethic, I already had in my head my brother's imita-tions. When my dad was talking to me about this stuff, it was as if he was performing a script that my brother had already written. This drew the sting out of anything that my father said to me. To be abso-lutely fair, though, my father often saw the funny side too. My brother started to do these imitations in front of the family and our father would say things like, 'I must try harder to sound like that . . .' and would even imitate my brother imitating him! In other words, my brother had succeeded in taking a lot of the tension out of the situation – in particular when any of it was directed at me.

But what effect did it have on my brother? I began this chapter by saying that we all have voices in our heads, and our father's voice is a very strong one for both me and my brother. In our seventies, as we are now, when we meet up it doesn't take long for one of us to do an imitation of something our father said. I've been doing some of these in my family show for the last 45 years! Even so, every now and then my brother shows me that our father's disapproval of things that he cared a lot about still saddens and puzzles him. Parental disapproval is a heavy weight to carry, and I am full of admiration for my brother finding a way to relieve himself, and me, of some of the burden.

I have another way of relieving that burden: rather than carrying the sense of failure that my father's words could sometimes give me, I ask why he was like that. Why was he so anxious that my brother and I should do better, even though by all accounts we were actually doing very well? And why wasn't he just content with doing all the thousands of positive, kind, loving, informative, mind-expanding things he did for us? I won't go into details, but just imagine us, say, being taken round tiny country churches and having ancient wood carvings being pointed out to us, or him coming again and again to see me in swimming competitions or rugby matches. He was tireless in how he supported us through our childhoods.

Let me expand on what I've mentioned earlier: my father was born in the US but was brought to London by his mother when he was two. He came with his older sister, who he was very fond of, and a younger brother, who died soon after. They moved into the tiny house where his maternal grandparents lived, along with his mother's sisters and brother. At one point, I think there were 11 people living in a two-up two-down terrace house in Whitechapel, behind Royal London Hospital. My father's mother couldn't work very easily because she had had polio and one of her arms was very weak as a result.

In the cramped, tense conditions of that home, my father dreamed that one day his American father would arrive on a white horse and save him from it all. But his father never wrote, never came, never asked him to come to the States to see him. When we were growing up, he would talk about it, sometimes make light of it, doing funny 'impressions' of the mix of English and Yiddish going on in that crowded household. Years later, though, he wrote about it and told the story with a tinge of sadness. In my forties I went to the States myself, and spent many hours with my father's cousin while he talked about my father's father, who had by then died in Boston's largest mental institution. When I came back, I had a whole pack of stories to tell my father about his father – his suits, his voice, a mysterious child (!), the row house – or terraced house – where my father had lived as a baby, the events on the day the family split up. I even had a photo of my father's father's gravestone, because I had visited it. When I started to tell my father about these things, I quickly realised that he didn't really want to know. He heard them out but with no great interest, nor any follow-up questions.

It's probably obvious by now, but I'll say it anyway. From this poverty-stricken beginning with such emotionally difficult goings-on, he became an educated – and brilliant – man. He was a teacher, then a teacher-trainer, did a PhD, became a professor and wrote a string of papers and books. You might say that his progress owed everything to education. If you wanted to be a bit more nuanced, you could say that he owed it all to the fact that his family (especially his mother and his mother's father) enabled him to 'get' what education is all about. It was an incredible achievement.

Now let's jump forward a bit, to me and my brother growing up. He clearly thought that if we didn't grab what education had to offer, we could end up in the gutter. There was even a thing that both my mother and father would say whenever either of them thought that we weren't working hard enough:

'You don't want to end up like the Michaelsons!' We had never met the Michaelsons. In fact, we didn't know anything about the Michaelsons other than what my parents used as a cautionary tale. On one occasion, my mother did explain that the Michaelsons were very, very poor. They lived in a mysterious place called a 'tenement' (I had never seen a tenement!), and the only job that Mr Michaelson could get was as a 'shlepper' – that's the guy who helps the market trader take stuff to and from his stall. 'All he had was a wheelbarrow!'

I don't think there was ever going to be even the faintest chance that either my brother or I was going to end up being 'like the Michaelsons'. I don't mean that in any arrogant way, but our parents did so much to open our eyes to books, films, plays, poems, history, architecture, nature, science and politics that some of it was going to come out somewhere, somehow, no matter what ups and downs we faced at school. But that one phrase – 'You don't want to end up like the Michaelsons' – tells me a lot. My parents were anxious. They both came from migrant families who had suffered persecution and hardship. They had lived through the horror of the Holocaust when relatives in France and Poland had 'disappeared'. They had both moved from poverty to the secure teaching jobs and they owed it all, as they saw it, to education.

My father in particular couldn't stop himself

passing on his worry that somehow or other my brother or I could slip back to where they had come from. Woven into that worry was the fact that my father had no father, while we had all the luck of having one who provided for us, looked out for us, and filled our heads full of jokes, stories, knowledge, and intellectual stimuli. In some very odd way, could our father have been envious of the fact that we had a father? Even though the father we had was him?! Was that the edge that came with all that badgering of us about our As?

I find this way of thinking helpful. I've gone from feeling bad, feeling not good enough, fed up that I had disappointed my father to a feeling of satisfaction that I have explained things to myself. It doesn't necessarily end with a conclusion that wraps everything up, but it gives me a place to go whenever I think about me, my brother and my father in the car pulling out of Victoria Station. Yes, he was someone who thought that by telling us that we weren't 'good enough', we would try harder and get better. Sometimes that made me feel bad, but I can now think that his insistence on doing so was much more about him than us.

As I said at the beginning of this Victoria Station story, I hoped that if I told you the backstory it would give you a blueprint for examining your own story, one you hold in your head as a moment of deflation, or worse. We can dig into these stories and figure out why people said or did certain things. I think that when we do this, it frees us from the power the story once held over us, it's ability to hurt us. Instead, we take control of the story and tell it our way. And something else: parts of the backstories we tell can become little shorthand catchphrases. If I think of my father wishing that I had done better at my exams, I can just say to myself, 'You don't want to end up like the Michaelsons!' and that's like a magic shorthand, whipping me back to thinking of my parents trying to navigate their way through their lives from poverty to comfort. My moment of feeling bad fades.

I want to finish this chapter by looking at a knock-back – not a killer blow, but the kind of knock-back that is part of working life for most people. I'm including this here because working life carries a lot forwards from school and college life. Apart from anything else, the set-up is very similar: you have to do work for someone else, you get watched, marked and if you screw up, you get disciplined. In fact, how we behave in the workplace is often learned before we get there and it comes from our time at school.

Here's the situation: I was working for the BBC, presenting a radio programme about children's books (again, very much related to school and education!). I realise I'm talking about something which in the general run of things is hugely privileged and I'm not going to pretend – poor me – this is like working long hours on low pay in an office or factory, where the stresses are very different. Even so, I think it might ring some bells.

A small group of us, working together on this job, started building up a good routine and team spirit. The show had been going for a few years, and top writers wanted to come on to the programme to talk about their books. I had found a way to ask them questions which (so they told me) they found stimulating and the feedback from listeners was over-whelmingly nice. I was becoming quite proud that we were the only outlet on any UK radio or TV channel that talked about children's books in a way that was both serious and fun, got people thinking about what makes for a good (or bad) children's book and at the same time helped people choose books for their children. Fatal mistake! Never get so proud, or confident, that you think you'll be there doing it next summer!

Quite suddenly, out of the blue, we got a note from on high which said that the 'controller' of the radio channel was taking us off air. No reason was given. I immediately thought that it was my fault. I must have done something wrong, or it must have been decided that my face didn't fit. Or my voice, more like! Perhaps you recognise this: self-blame as explanation for any knock-back. Perhaps, too, there was a bit of 'impostor syndrome' – telling myself that I didn't fit or that I wasn't really entitled to be there anyway.

We made enquiries. It turned out that a new boss had come in and he wanted to make some changes. He had identified our programme as 'ghetto programming', as he called it. What's that, you might ask? He explained that he didn't like programmes which were aimed at a 'single interest group'. I looked at the schedule: to my eyes it was full of programmes for single interest groups and the channel was all the stronger for it. That's because, as a listener, you could stray outside of your own particular interest group and eavesdrop on people talking about stuff that wasn't on your patch.

Our team made this point to the new boss. He brushed it aside and that was that. To tell the honest truth, I was devastated. Not in the same way as a loss of a loved one or a dreadful accident, but nevertheless, I felt it as a professional knock-back. I had become, in a way, so confident that we were doing a good job that I had become too confident. A bit smug, perhaps. I had thought we were part of the furniture. And now we were the old wardrobe, chucked in a skip. Even though the boss gave us his explanation, and it wasn't personal, I felt personally rejected – a bit humiliated, even. Deep down, I really did continue to think it was my fault. My line of thinking was that if I had been really, really brilliant at the job, the boss wouldn't have been able to give us the chop even if he had wanted to.

So I sulked. In other words, I didn't know what to do with the knock-back, the put-down, so I absorbed it.

Then two things happened, both of which were out of my control. The boss left, and I was asked to present another radio programme. I mention the boss (let's call him Roger) leaving because it gave me an excuse. We all love an excuse. Excuses are our alibis, our get-out clauses. What I told myself was that Roger hadn't been really committed to the job. (I'm not saying that this is true, it's just the story that I told myself to feel better about myself.) In my mind, I went on: Roger had wanted to be a new broom, put on a bit of a show, to prove to someone even higher than him that he meant business and so had to show that he could make heads roll, clear out the dead wood. Saying all this to myself was magic. It took the burden off me, and I no longer felt I was the one to blame. I now had a whole story to use to explain it away. I had 'rationalised' it, as the jargon puts it. Or, I had 'displaced' my anger about myself and focussed it on Roger. And what a relief it was. It really is one way to get better!

Now, I'm going to be cautious about recommending this for all knock-backs and put-downs. It's easy to make a mistake and use this method for escaping blame or dodging responsibility. But there are times when you can see that the reason why you've 'failed' is because of structures bigger than yourself. That your 'failure' is not because *you* are a failure but because the cogs of the machine that you're in have turned and squeezed you out.

Unlike millions of others, I'm not telling a story about being made unemployed. I wasn't out on the street, panicking about how I was going to support my family, pay the rent or mortgage, or fill my days. It's a far cry from the kind of life-changing blow that has hit many others, but nevertheless we all encounter minor challenges that can hit us surprisingly hard. I hope that performing the same mind shift – focussing on the wider cause of your apparent downfall – might help you too.

And then I got the best of all possible ways out of the hole I was in: I got offered another job. There is of course no better way for your ego to recover than for something new to come along, especially if they say that they want you to do the very thing you were rejected for. (Or thought you were rejected for.)

Why though? Why did I get that offer? I told myself that one reason for it was that I must have done well in the previous job after all, presenting the programme about children's books. Them 'up there' liked it. My voice did fit after all. It set me thinking about the stuff I did at school and university, not just the knowledge I had accrued but all the things I had done, like acting in plays, doing research on projects, writing articles and books. When I considered these things, I felt OK about saying to myself that I had earned it. I know that in a way that's an arrogant or 'entitled' thing for me to say. But I'm saying it because what I've done here is gather up my 'stuff' – a CV, if you like – and put it out there in the shop window. Thinking in that way, you can begin to feel more confident. I'm no great expert on career guidance, but in the experience I have of helping people, I have found that many people are incredibly good at underselling themselves, underestimating what they've done, reluctant to see that the mix of education, work and life that they've experienced is worth something. This is not about boasting, or fibbing that you've done stuff that you haven't done. It's about being willing to gather together all the bits and pieces of your life and put it out there in a package, one that gets people to take a look at you.

And if you find that there are gaps or holes in this package, then you can ask yourself, what can I do to fill them? Once again, education can be the answer. And it isn't just for the very young! In my forties, I was overcome by a feeling that I had cut short my education: I hadn't learned as much as I could. It really bothered me that I had studied a bit of French but then dropped it. It started to annoy me and even made me sad. This can be a dangerous state of mind:

in this mood, it can be very easy to blame the people around you for why you're not expanding your mind, or getting better at something. I'm not going to pretend that I didn't paint myself into that corner, but I did jump out of it: I enrolled on an evening class in French. This turned out to be one of the most exciting bits of education I have ever done. All I did was turn up one evening a week for a year. We sat in class – a very diverse group of people, speaking French, talking about books, films, music. We had homework, and came into the class prepared to talk about what we had read. This may not be everyone's cup of tea but I can tell you that learning new things sent my mind whizzing. I felt alive. Learning new things has the power to change us.

Off the back of that evening class, at the age of 45, I enrolled on a part-time master's degree.

It changed my direction of travel. Instead of trying to busk everything, I started to build up a genuine expertise. I got myself up to speed with new ideas and new research. It was very exciting. I felt that I was in something rather than being outside looking in. It was a tonic. Doing some research, writing it up, discussing it with fellow students and tutors felt like a breath of fresh air.

All this confirmed for me something I probably knew anyway: education is for life. I saw my parents doing this with evening classes, diplomas, MAs and

PhDs. And I've done the same. It's not easy to find the time, motivation, or money, but if you can, it's a liberator. It makes you grow, it makes you stand up. It makes you feel good because you discover a 'can-do' in yourself. And it's never too late to do it. I've seen people in their seventies and eighties do master's degrees and doctorates. I've seen people taking up cooking, wood-carving, painting – anything. And you can start anywhere.

Thinking about my evening classes makes me feel really good. It's a feeling I treasure and always will, and it proves that 'getting better' at whatever you choose to pursue is something you can spend your whole life enjoying.

Chapter 6

Go next year, they won't have banned the bomb by then!

When I was 14 I ran away from home. OK, that's an exaggeration. What I did was go away for a few days, even though my parents said that I shouldn't. This was in the early 1960s. The talk was of 'The Bomb'. Atom bombs, nuclear bombs, nuclear tests and the nuclear deterrent. People were reminding themselves – and young people like me – of what happened at Hiroshima and Nagasaki. Was it possible that great-power rivalry could lead to an all-out nuclear war which would wipe out the human race? Was nuclear testing causing terrible damage to people right here and now – cancers especially? And why was Britain spending all this money on nuclear arms when other countries of a similar size were not? Couldn't we spend that money on houses, schools, the transport system and hospitals?

All those questions were bundled into a movement called 'Ban the Bomb'. There were marches, demonstrations, songs, poems and other performances. I wanted to be part of it, so I announced to my parents, 'I'm going on the Aldermaston March to ban the bomb.' This was a four-day march from a nuclear weapons test centre near the town of Aldermaston in Buckinghamshire to Trafalgar Square, London. I wanted to do the whole thing. I wanted to be part of it.

My parents' reaction was immediate.

My father said, 'It's out of the question.' He turned to my mother, 'The boy's mad. Meshugge [Yiddish for crazy].'

My mother's response was typical: 'Where will you stay? You'd have nothing to eat. You don't know anyone. What would you eat? You're not going. Harold, say something! He's too young. Look at him, he's packing. You can't go without a spare pair of trousers. How can he carry a bag like that for twenty miles a day? Stop him, Harold. What will you do in the evening? You need to eat. You get ill if you don't eat. Take a tin of beans. You can always eat beans. Harold, stop him. There's the chicken! Take the chicken. If you're taking a tin of beans, take two. He's 14, Harold. Go next year. Wait till next year.

They won't have banned the bomb by then, believe me. There'll be another march. Go on that one. You must keep eating fresh fruit. And you like dates. He's always liked dates, hasn't he, Harold? Just squeeze them in down the side of the bag. Couldn't he wait till the last day, when we'll be there? We can all go to Trafalgar Square together. Harold, have you got the chicken? Just because it's Easter, doesn't mean it's warm. It can snow at Easter. Wear the string vest. Who's organised the coaches? Do we know these people, Harold? One orange?! Take five. And raisins. He's 14. It's ridiculous. He can't go. Keep the chicken wrapped. Phone us if you need more food. Goodbye.'

That's how my mother stopped me from going on the Aldermaston March in 1961. That's to say, she didn't stop me at all!

When I look back at that moment, I can see that I was doing several things at the same time: I had decided that the world was going in the wrong direction and I would do something about it. I also decided that I didn't want to just be a hanger-on to my parents when, in their own rather boring way (as I saw it), they had themselves decided they would go along, but only on the last day. Oh no, I was going to have the adventure of doing the whole march, over four days, sleeping on school floors and in giant marquees, listening to jazz, hearing protest songs and poems – being this new kind of person. The word hippie hadn't quite arrived in London, but I wanted to be one of those ban-the-bomb types.

Whether you have any sympathy with that far-off 14-year-old me or not, you can at the very least see that I was someone who wanted to do something. I thought that by joining in with thousands of others, things might change for the better. Political parties or governments, I thought, would change their minds. When I see the climate change protests today, they remind me very much of that Aldermaston March. They too involve taking on the fate of the whole planet, while at the same time encouraging people to change their lifestyle – how we look, how we eat, how and who we love, what music we like.

I don't want to get into a discussion here about whether I and the others on that march were right or wrong, nor whether climate change protestors are right or wrong now. I'll leave that for another time. I'm making a different point, about what it feels like to think about how the human race is going to survive, and then to join other people and feel as if you're doing something that you care about and have become committed to. If you want, you can think of yourself as a cog, and all the other people you're joining are cogs that mesh with you. You turn, they turn. They turn, you turn. You feel as if you're making things better 'out there', which can make you feel better 'in here', in your own mind.

In this chapter, I'm moving away from thinking about 'getting better' as a thing you do on your own, for yourself, and looking at it in the context of how we are in the world. Sometimes we're in disagreement with the world, and sometimes we might think the world is in disagreement with us, but with both feelings comes a chance to get better.

In response to those feelings, I've taken part in many different kinds of protest and campaigns, although mostly I don't join political parties. I've lived long enough to see some of these campaigns fail and some succeed. When they fail, you have to do some hard thinking: did it fail because the issue was wrong – in other words 'we were wrong'? Did it fail because the campaign was conducted the wrong way? Did it fail because there was something wrong with the leaders? Or were most of the people in the campaign wrong? If we were right, why didn't the world wake up and agree with us? Or was it the way 'the media' ignored us, or told lies about us? All these questions push you into thinking a lot about what society is, and how things can get better. It can also make you look inwards and ask yourself what you're doing by getting involved. And that's tough if the campaign fails. You might be left saying to yourself, what was all that for?

One answer to this is that it's better to have done something rather than nothing. Another looks back at terrible times in the middle of the twentieth century and says something along the lines of, 'For evil to prosper, all it needs is for good people to do nothing.' You can even look back through history and pick out people who stood for things, got together with others, lost in their own lifetimes but, we might say, history has been kind to them – it's proved them right. For example, there was the fight for women's suffrage. Hundreds of thousands of women took part in campaigns to win the vote, even though many died before it came to pass. What do we say then, across time, to those women who died before they won anything? That they had failed? That their battle to win was pointless because they did not benefit from it directly, or immediately? Absolutely not: they were part of a movement that drove change.

The phrase 'protest and survive' (or 'protest to survive') emerged in the Ban the Bomb era. It was a parody of the British government's slogan and leaflet 'Protect and Survive', which seemed to suggest that we could survive a nuclear war. Or even more seriously, that 'we' (whoever that is) could *win* a nuclear war. When Edward Thompson came up with the slogan 'protest and survive', he suggested that telling people they could survive was one way the government was actually leading us into a nuclear war, by kidding us that we would survive and win, while in actual fact the human race as a whole would lose – a terrifying thought.

'Protest and survive' and 'protest to survive' are brilliantly effective slogans partly because, to me at least, they suggest that protesting in itself is a way of surviving.

Let's chew that one over for a moment. At any time, you might think life is unfair, or life hasn't treated you well, or you deserve better, or that the way things are discriminates against people (you or others like you), or that you can't be yourself because 'society' won't let you. This doesn't apply to situations where you might want to dominate or exploit others, of course: the cluster of feelings and thoughts I'm talking about here are where the unfairness is not only something 'out there' but also felt inside. If any of this rings a bell, then the phrase 'protest to survive' has another meaning. It means that you can feel through protesting that you can resist the pressure coming from 'out there' and also feel empowered within yourself.

If that all sounds very abstract, to better grasp it you only have to listen to gay people talking about how they felt growing up in my lifetime, where all the talk around them seemed to deny their right to be who they were. As I wrote this chapter, many people were commenting on the fact that the finalists for 2021's *Strictly Come Dancing* included a deaf woman, a woman of colour and two gay men. As ever, the dancing was a powerful expression of passion, love, coordination, cooperation, strength and belief, and several of the dancers wanted to say that they wished that they had been able to see people like them doing such things when they were growing up. They were saying that, when they were younger, 'out there' had made things hard for them 'in here'.

The roads that led to achieving this kind of representation are full of the most incredible battles, sacrifices, protests, defeats, minor victories, setbacks, and, finally, big victories. We might say, in the context of this book, that the *Strictly Come Dancing* final was a moment when things got a bit better. Some might say that *Strictly* is just 'spectacle', that it can't and won't change people's lives and won't change the minds of those people who are prejudiced. That's a negative approach, and says that things can't and shouldn't get better. In reality, these small steps, made by individuals, make a big difference.

One way to get a bit of perspective on all this is to think about our parents and grandparents.

My grandmother and mother fought for the vote and equal pay. My forbears' stories are full of times when they struggled with the world around them. When I went to see my father's cousin, Ted, in America, he told me something that made me think. His parents were immigrants to the US from Poland and Latvia. They were very poor but Ted was good at school and applied to universities to study medicine. He quickly discovered that most of the medical schools had what was called a 'Jewish quota'. That is, they would only accept a fixed number of Jewish students.

He wrote about this in his memoir:

The first hospital rejected me completely. The notification read as follows; 'The committee on interns has met and has decided that it was for the good of the hospital that others than you should be chosen.'

Just that one sentence and nothing more.

I judged it to be a very carefully crafted sentence and the message was clear again – No Jews here. The letter was signed by a name I shall never forget. It was the same name as a town in Massachusetts. I read that letter over and over again and again during the next few days. I thought of it when I went to bed and when I got up. I thought about it at night, as I lay awake. I thought about it as I went about with my hospital training. But I never mentioned receiving that letter to anyone, not to my friends and certainly not to my parents.

Eventually, I tore the letter up and discarded it. Even though the letter was gone, its content has always remained with me. But its content remained my secret. I told no one, not even my wife Gladys until some time in the middle of the 1960s when we were talking deeply about anti-Semitism.

Fuelled by this, my father's cousin decided not to apply to some of the top colleges in the US, including Harvard.

Can you feel the sadness and pain in his words, and the fact that he kept the letter secret for more than 30 years? He did tell his mother that he was turning down a chance to apply to go to Harvard. She was horrified. What was he thinking of? It was a chance in a lifetime, the first like it for anyone in the family and a chance to become one of the country's top doctors! No matter, he stuck to his guns and went to study where there were no quotas.

Was he right?

Did he sacrifice a chance for himself to 'get better' for the sake of a point of principle? And what was that principle? That he shouldn't have to go somewhere where staff or students would be prejudiced against him? Or something bigger than this – that colleges shouldn't discriminate? OK, but did his one-man boycott make that bigger situation better? He may have been one man, but if many individuals come together and stick to their guns, they can be part of change over time. In that sense, maybe cousin Ted was an active part of making things better. In his own way, maybe he was one tiny part of something that eventually became the civil rights movement, which in turn paved the way for movements of today, like Black Lives Matter. What's more certain, because Ted told me as much, is that he was proud of not applying for Harvard and of why he did it, though there were times he wondered if, from a purely selfish point of view, he had done the right thing.

I often say to myself that we have to gather up the things that make us proud. We can do it quietly, on our own, in our minds. It might be a big or a small thing but being proud of something we've done is a very large part of how we hold ourselves together, how we find a purpose for what we do, and it's a very large part too of feeling good – or better.

My parents loved to tell us the story of 'Cable Street'. These days it's usually called the Battle of Cable Street, but that wasn't what it was called when our parents told the story, usually at the tea table in our flat in Pinner. The leader of the British Union of Fascists, Oswald Mosley, announced that on 4 October 1936, he was going to lead a march of the BUF down Cable Street in London's East End. At that time, Cable Street and the area around it was a largely Jewish quarter. When the day came, several hundred thousand protestors stood in the way of where the march was going to go. For hours, the police charged at the protestors, trying to forge a way through, but in the end they failed. The march didn't happen. My parents were only 17 at the time, and my father lived very near to Cable Street. They were both there, together, on that day.

I can see now that it was something that my mother in particular was proud of. I could also see that it made her feel good to tell us about it. Perhaps it even surprised her that she was telling us. After all, we were growing up in a time and place that could almost have been on the other side of the Earth from where she grew up. It was so different from what it had been like for her. My father painted the picture of how risky and dangerous it felt, when they were young, to be walking from where he lived in the largely Jewish quarter to where our mother lived in a largely non-Jewish area. Mum would laugh at him overdramatising the story, but then tell us stories of how people she knew had been attacked by 'Mosley's lot' – the British Union of Fascists, which certainly suggested that things had been dangerous for her.

How do you feel better, or force change, when you find yourself facing such things? Unfortunately it's not a question I ever asked my parents, who for a few years must have felt as if the whole world was closing in on them: Spain, Germany, the people in high places in Britain who wanted to 'appease' Hitler, and then Mosley's lot on the streets where they lived. There were also the sly comments that teachers might make about Jewish kids being too clever for their own good or articles in newspapers blaring out at them.

One popular daily newspaper even ran the headline 'Hurrah for the Blackshirts!' (the uniform worn by the British Union of Fascists). Both my parents did a lot of things to resist internalising such things. One way, a very important one, was to resist being people who blamed themselves for the prejudice that was directed towards them. They both found refuge and progress in the education offered them by the East End state schools they went to. It made them proud that they did well. But they were also proud that they resisted the prejudice more directly at Cable Street.

When my parents told the story of that day, they filled it with detail: about seeing their friends getting hurt, running down side streets, getting trapped in a cul-de-sac with mounted police coming towards them, a kind person opening a door and taking them in. I also came to realise that this day had an extra special meaning for my parents: it would have been one of the first times they were out on their own together. Quite a first date!

Hearing such stories from your parents is a very warm, reassuring thing. And the feeling lasts. Such things are part of a chain of being – the circle of life, if you like. And even if we miss out on it from our own parents, we can give it to our children. I was very lucky to be asked by Channel 5 to contribute to a documentary on the Battle of Cable Street in 2019. I told the story my parents had told me and Channel

5 matched archive footage to it. But then, quite suddenly, I noticed something that I had never heard about before. You see, it was always said that the 'battle' on that day was not between Mosley's lot and East Enders. Mosley's lot, people said, had been kept a few hundred yards away from the crowd, until the way had been cleared for them to come through. As I said, this never happened, they never did come through. But now, looking at this film, I could see something very clearly: a guy in the uniform of the British Union of Fascists was standing next to a policeman, lashing out at the demonstrators, then stepping back while a policeman whacked the demonstrator with his baton. They were taking it in turns! I had the sudden satisfaction of seeing another view of what took place. I was there doing that commentary only because someone had heard me talk about my parents' telling me the story of Cable Street. I found myself in this circle of life created by the proud telling of family stories, just as my parents had found strength in collective action that day. Then, as part of that chain of being, I can tell that story to my children.

There was, of course, an alternative view to the one that said, 'Come out on to the streets to stop Mosley marching.' That alternative view said that people should stay indoors, draw the curtains and wait till it blew over. As I was growing up, I didn't ever meet anyone who did that, so I can't gauge how that choice felt, either at the time or down through the years. I guess that my parents went out on the streets because they didn't want to give in. They didn't want to concede the physical space of their streets nor the mental space in their heads to Mosley's lot. When they achieved that, they felt better.

Watching the films for Channel 5, though, filled me with other feelings: anger, sadness, and again pride that my parents had stood up to this stuff and here I was talking about it on their behalf, on telly. Of course, I know that only very few people get the privilege of being 'heard' like this. And it's said over and over again that there are millions of people who feel that they don't get 'heard'. Some say that's the explanation for why the Brexit vote went the way that it did: for millions it felt like the first time they had a chance to say something quickly, simply and directly. I have no idea if that's true, but I know that people are often very keen to be heard and acknowledged by others. I've noticed that during the course of my work, if I sit with people for more than just a few minutes, the slightest trigger can set them off telling stories of what pains them, what's been difficult for them, what has made them proud about the way they overcame a difficulty. I see people – like my parents – reliving these moments full of emotion, their eyes full of concentration, beaming or watering. I think this is the core of what makes us human.

When we can't be part of a circle of talking and listening, we suffer. We find it difficult to feel valued. When we are heard, and we feel that as a result we are part of something, things feel better, even if our circumstances remain challenging.

Now for something a bit more recent. In 2021, a 3.5 metre-tall living artwork of a young Syrian refugee child called *Little Amal* 'walked' across Turkey, Greece, Italy, France, Switzerland, Germany, Belgium and the UK to focus attention on refugees. She was in effect a giant doll or puppet, operated by several people holding ropes. They walked Amal 8,000 kilometres.

I'll declare an interest. On one of the days she was in London, I was asked, along with other poets, artists, dancers, singers, politicians and religious leaders, to welcome her. I was invited to read one or two poems.

What was the point of it all? I asked myself. A great long walk, full of difficulty, some real hardship for the people walking the giant puppet, all ending up with no action or result. The doll itself was an odd but very beautiful sight. She appeared to look out over the crowds with a serene certainty. But what did it tell us? And what did it do for refugees? More specifically, what did it do for people who think we should do more to help refugees and what did it do about those who think we do too much and the only thing we should be doing is turning them away?

I don't actually have any answers to these questions, but I can say that I found being there on the day moving. As I listened on the radio to the organisers describing where they had been and how they had been received along the way, I had a sense of the great many conversations that must have taken place in people's homes, in the streets, in shops and cafes, and in schools and colleges along the route *Little Amal* took. *Little Amal* sparked these. Even if it was only for a few minutes, the *Little Amal* event would have, at the very least, asked people not to turn away from what has become an international crisis. For those few minutes, Amal represented the thousands of people on the move, fleeing from war, poverty, famine and disease. It's really much easier to put such things out of sight, out of mind, to tell yourself that you didn't cause the war, poverty, famine or disease, so why should you pick up the pieces? But then, thinking of myself, I only have to spend a little time reading and it's not long before I discover that in fact the country where I vote and pay my taxes is tied into many of the things that have resulted in hardship and terror for people 'over there'.

So on the one hand, *Little Amal* was just a gesture – what hostile people might call one great big bit of 'virtue signalling' – and on the other she was a cunning bit of provocation, a bit of stirring that got many of us thinking. In all honesty, I keep asking myself, did that giant walk make things better? Will it make it more likely that we can solve the problem that *Little Amal* was highlighting? I can't answer that question because it's too soon to know. We'll have a better idea in the coming years, as we see how attitudes towards refugees change (or don't). But in that moment, all of us who were there watching *Little Amal* shared in a moving moment, one that told us there was a possibility of action, and of change.

And here writing in a book about such things precisely because *Little Amal* came past me! In that sense, it worked too: the message is passed on.

I'd like to finish this chapter with another situation that has struck me recently, this time one that happens in a place of work. Managers manage. Sometimes that means that it's their job to make sure that we work longer, or for less money, or both. There are hundreds of different ways for them to do this: wage freezes, wage cuts, zero-hour contracts, redundancies, casualisation, short-term contracts, no overtime rates and so on. For all my life, I've seen people in many walks of life struggling to cope with this: teachers, nurses, miners, railway workers. As I'm writing this, it's happening to my colleagues and me in our place of work, a university. For the first time in my life, I'm right in the middle of a dispute. I'm a union member and our union is doing what it can to oppose the cuts, casualisation and redundancies being imposed on us. As with Cable Street I can ask the question, what would it be like to do nothing? What would it be like to sit back and let the management sack all the people they want to sack, close down all the departments they want to close?

At one level, it's easy to answer that: hardship and difficulty for scores of people. These are people who have spent years building up their qualifications, skills and experience, creating departments with years of collective know-how and at the stroke of a pen, it's all become worthless. There is no guarantee that any of them will get a job somewhere else.

There is also another level, to do with education and what we offer young people. Decisions are being made that will close down young people's chances to explore the areas that the university has decided don't matter.

The main way we have to resist these attacks is through a trade union.

When there are such conflicts, there are questions like: 'How will I earn a living?' and 'How will I pay my bills this week?' But there are bigger questions too, about what kind of society we want. Do we want to stand by while opportunities and freedoms are eroded? This is where union action, and strikes, come into their own. If you take part in the activities organised to resist cuts and redundancies, you avoid feeling isolated, you avoid blaming yourself for what is being done to you and your colleagues, and you get to see yourself as an active 'agent' in your own life. You become someone doing things, rather than someone having things done to them; active instead of passive; collective rather than individual. And sometimes, you might even change the outcome! But even if that is not always possible, there is power in the process.

As I write these things down, I don't know where we've got to with our own dispute. Management (apparently under guidance from the banks who have taken over the university) has delivered humiliating notices to some members of staff, telling them that either they've been fired or will be fired as part of the restructuring. We've been on strike. No one knows what will happen next. All the people I talk to want to go on making the sacrifices that are needed in order to try to prevent management from doing this. All the people I talk to are trying to make things better for the people in the firing line, better for the college, better for education.

And it's not easy. Some of us think that we are a proving ground, a trial run, if you like. Universities all over the education system are going through (or will go through) similar situations. For the moment it can seem like this is about a few people's jobs, but it's really become about the kind of big questions I mentioned earlier: what are universities for, and who should run them? In our case, the big decisions are now being made by bankers. Bankers? Yes, indeed! We ask ourselves, do people out there realise what is happening? We've devoted our lives to making universities better and here they are being made worse. So, we are coming together to defend our principles, and we hope that we have more strength if we do this together. We are in a struggle to make things better.

One of the enemies of feeling better is feeling lonely. That's a pretty obvious thing to say, but if I pose myself a couple of related questions – what did it feel like being lonely? When you were lonely, how did you get out of it? – I can surprise myself with what I find. In my case, thinking about these questions often takes me back to my childhood, and then it's as if all the lonely moments between then and now join up. I think that's because even if the situations in which we feel lonely might be hugely different, the actual feeling seems to remain the same. I can remember what it felt like walking down the suburban streets where we lived, especially just as it was getting dark. In those days, in the fifties, a lot of people thought it was a bit vulgar to have lights on with curtains open at the front of their houses. As a result, long suburban roads could feel empty and closed. I used to think it was as if the houses' eyes were shut. Quite often there would be no one in the street either, so I was both alone and lonely. The feeling I had then is no different from the one I had lying in my bed in the geriatric ward, not being able to talk to other patients, not being able to talk to anyone at home, no nurses or doctors coming by just at that moment. More than 60 years between the two experiences, and yet the feeling is the same.

I find it helpful to think about loneliness. To be honest, I think I'm a bit afraid of it. I work out ways in which I can avoid it, or as I sometimes say, 'beat' it. That's probably a bit daft, because the moment you see something as a fight, you set up winners and losers. My wife is a genius at creating 'cosy'. Cosy is opposed to loneliness. The way she does it is to create places around us that we can feel good about. It's obvious really, and I guess most of us try to do this at some time or another, but some people certainly have a knack for it. The nearest I get to creating a cosy place is the space where I work. To others, it looks a mess. For me, it's surrounded with 'friends': bits and bobs, objects, boxes, shelves, surfaces covered in things that I treasure. Each thing links me to a moment or a person, either from the past or in my life now. The desk I work at has got old stones from holidays, my adult children's LEGO-people they had thirty or forty years ago, juggling cubes I once used to learn how to juggle. Stacked up in a corner are boxes full of my late son Eddie's books, shirts and note-books. In a folder, I've got some antique sheets and booklets that people used to buy in the street for their children, like the ballad of Tom Thumb from the early nineteenth century. I've loved collecting these. Maybe another word like 'cosy' is 'safe'. To have these things is to feel safe. When I think of my father's cousin Michael, I realise that all he had left from his home were a couple of photos and those letters. Once he left home, nearly everything he had or met was new – apart from his memories, of course.

Part of the struggle to get better is to not feel lonely. Is feeling lonely one step towards feeling hope-less or helpless? When we feel hopeless or helpless it's very, very hard to do the things we need to do to get better: exercise, stretching, eating good, fresh food, keeping clean and warm. Instead, when we're lonely or feeling helpless and hopeless, it's very easy to just sit on our bums all day, eat badly, not wash often enough, and – simple though it may sound – we avoid stretching our bodies in the way that cats do. Stretch-ing not only gets our blood circulating and strengthens our muscles, it also massages us inside. The more we do of it, the better we feel. I'm not saying stretching will stop you feeling lonely, more that loneliness can stop us doing things that will make us feel better.

The way most of us get rid of loneliness is by

being less alone, whether that's by being with family, friends, colleagues, or in convivial surroundings with strangers. One thing we've had to do during the pandemic is find other ways to do this: texting, emails, Zoom, Skype and social media. It's possible to use social media as a space to share the things we care about with whoever we want to share them with, and in doing so to feel less alone. The important thing is to find ways to make it work for you and whatever group you want to be in.

It's no substitute for the love and care of family, friends and people you care about, or who care about you or your project, work, or activity. But it sure can be a miracle if you want it to be. You can do serious sharing of ideas and feelings, you can use it to find out things, learn things or just 'enjoy the craic', having light-hearted banter with people who are not trying to do you down, or you do them down. It can be a way to push away loneliness and feel a little better.

Chapter 7

Just because I'm paranoid, doesn't mean that they're not out to get me

This chapter is about paranoia. Well, two types of paranoia actually: the one where you imagine that people are out to get you and the other that is real because people really *are* out to get you. But hang on, the experts say, the one that's real, that's not paranoia. True, but more on that later.

It's easy to be flippant about paranoia, telling someone 'Don't be so paranoid!', so long as you're not in the grip of it yourself. I often hear that gag, 'Just because I'm paranoid, doesn't mean that they're not out to get me.' Jokes like that relieve our worry and anxiety, but the snag with them is that they minimise the awful fix we get into if we are in the midst of paranoia. It is something I have faced myself, and is hard to pull yourself back from.

There was a point in my life when I was – how shall I put it? – seriously confused. One relationship had come to an end. (But had it *really* come to an end?) Shortly after, another relationship had also come to an end. (But had it, really?) You can't get much more confused than that. Was I giving mixed messages, or were the other people the ones giving me mixed messages? Tangled up with this were feelings on all sides of anger, betrayal and lashings of indecision, as is so often the case when relationships end. Hark back now to the chapter on my hypothyroidism, a time when I had a sense that I was silently cutting myself off from doing things but didn't yet know why. This 'point in my life', as I've called it, happened in the midway point of that illness.

This is a perfect storm: a whirlpool of emotions about people close to me, coinciding with mysterious deteriorations in my body. At some point, I started to stick anything that went wrong with me on to other people, people I was suspicious of. One example: I had a self-assembly bookcase propped up in the hallway of the flat where I was living. A guy I knew quite well came over and he leaned against the bookcase, so that it fell over and hundreds of books fell on the floor. He laughed. This really, really bothered me. Actually, I was desperately upset, and his laughter triggered something in me, as though the accident had been malicious, which in retrospect surely wasn't the case. Shortly after this incident, I remembered that he knew a chain of people in my life (the rational part of me should have said, 'Of course he does! That's how people live!'). Some of the people he knew were in the circle of people who were in this mess of mixed messages and betrayals. Then the paranoia kicked in: now I had what I felt was 'evidence': *These people were talking to each other,* I said to myself. *They were each, in their own way, finding ways to get at me.* I lay in bed mapping the networks between people: *Who knew who? How did so-and-so get to meet what's-his-name . . . and why?*

When very intimate relationships come to an end, it sets up an awkward and weird question: what will the person you used to be with say about you to their next partner? This gets extra awkward and weird if their next partner is someone you know well . . . *They've both got a dossier on me!* Well, you might think this, if you're in a paranoid frame of mind. And it might not even be a matter of the next relationship. It might just be a meeting – two people who only know each other through you, meet up. *Arrggghhh! It's a conspiracy. It's a plot.*

How to deal with this?

The problem with paranoia is that, at the time, it feels real. After all, what are thoughts? Some of them are about totally verifiable facts: I wash the dishes. I go into another room. I ask myself, *Did I wash the dishes? Yes, I washed the dishes. Why am I wondering if I washed the dishes?* We have thoughts like these all the time. They're little circuits of memory and commentary; commentary and memory; round and round and round. The problem with the paranoid stuff is that it doesn't actually feel any different from a very ordinary, everyday set of thoughts like my washing-dishes circuit. *He pulled the bookcase over. He laughed. He asked me for Jim's phone number. Jim went out with Mo. Mo made that cutting remark about me in front of everyone.* In other words, it's a very small jump from having rational thoughts where you just wonder about something very ordinary to paranoid and destructive thoughts.

When you're inside this circuit, everything is proof of anything. Anything can be made to prove something. And it's totally and absurdly egotistical. It's all about an imaginary world in which the picture you have of your big 'me' in your mind is of huge importance to a whole group of people. It's as if the 'me' thinks of itself as Julius Caesar and all my best friends (and friends of my best friends) are plotting to stab me to death. Most of us, though, are not Julius Caesar. If we set up scenarios of conspirators, we are setting ourselves up to be Caesars. We are inflating ourselves. After all, most of the time other people are too busy with their own lives to be thinking about us, let alone plotting our downfall.

There came a point where I felt I had to stop doing this to myself. I'm not sure what triggered this in me but I've known others to do it by physically moving to another city or moving from city to the country. One of the first steps I took to get me out of this 'circuit' was to try to remind myself how insignificant I was. I wasn't Caesar. Another was to remind myself that my thoughts belonged to something bigger even than egotism: narcissism, a self-regard where wanting people to admire me or like me was more important than anything else. What's weird about narcissism is that it doesn't have much to do with whether you yourself think you're good! It's not the same as vanity. Narcissism is about a need. It's not about an idea of yourself. It was a breakthrough for me to realise that paranoia was linked so closely to narcissism. For me, I reached that breakthrough by talking to my father and stepmother. This wasn't a conversation that was directly about paranoia or narcissism – the opposite, in fact. What I mean is that spending a few hours with them reminded me what life was like outside of the 'circuit'. I could sit with them and look back at the ugly place I was in and it became smaller. It didn't matter and the only reason I thought it mattered was because I had put myself in the middle of it, as if I was the sun in the middle of the solar system.

Another step for me was to try to unpick the dif-ferences between two types of situation: one where I could say of myself, yes, it was me who had screwed up, and the other where I could say that someone had obstructed what I wanted to do. I made two lists: one of my screw-ups; the other of real, provable blocks from others. It showed me how much of what was going wrong was definitely down to me! It's a humbling way to lift the cloud of paranoia. After all, we're actually pretty good at screwing things up all by ourselves without getting help from others!

These kinds of self-reflection can be helpful checks on what's going on. Just doing it in your mind, however, may well be not enough. We can write things down, or if we have the time and money, we can find someone to talk to about it. Ideally, this should be someone 'neutral' who won't feed into your paranoid circuit, like a trusted friend or a medical professional. If you 'confess' all to someone in the group you're becoming suspicious of, you'll find very soon that you've put them in the circuit too, believing they're out to get you too!

I remember a story from my childhood, which starts with the fact my mum taught with a woman – let's call her Mrs Taylor. Every so often, my parents would invite her and her husband over for a meal. Mrs Taylor's husband, Tom, worked in a lithography engraving firm. At some point in the evening, Tom would start talking about goings-on at the firm. The engraving business is not the most obvious setting for a gripping drama, but he used to tell long tales, last-ing hours, about mysterious and sinister connections between the people above him in the firm. He was sure that they belonged to some kind of secret brotherhood and that this brotherhood had links to other firms. What's more, he said, drawing us in closer, if you didn't belong to this brotherhood – or even worse – if you refused to join them, then your chances at the firm or your whole life would be blighted. Shock! We glanced at each other as Tom brought these terrible thoughts into our living room.

Listening to Tom was like watching a gripping thriller on TV. Each time he came over, he was on the brink of exposing them. He would show the world what was really going on. It would soon be all over the papers. It would. It really would. But he never did. There never was the great Tom Taylor revelation.

To this day, I can see his gleaming eyes, peering at us through his glasses. And us sitting utterly trans-fixed by the story. I have no idea whether Tom was really on to something or whether it was all in his head, but the story shows that our own personal para-noid episodes don't live in isolation. They exist alongside other people's conspiracy stories which may or may not 'prove' that ours is true. This tells us that paranoid feelings are not purely private or indi-vidual. They are fed by (and shaped) by paranoid talk and activity right from the time of our childhood. It's like it's a language all of its own – in my case, the Tom Taylor language. If we become familiar with it when we're children, it can become a default position for us when we're older. In fact, if we have paranoid episodes, it's helpful to do some digging into our past and see whether we can find a store of paranoia tales sitting in the shadows of our mind, stoking up our paranoid tendencies. You've seen the process here: I've brought Tom into the light to help understand why I got locked into paranoid explanations for ordinary events.

As it happens, another of my parents' friends became enmeshed in a national scandal. He worked in what used to be familiarly called a 'borstal', a type of youth detention centre. You can see a fictional representation of one of these in Ray Winstone's second film, *Scum*, which showed the place to be brutal, violent, dangerous and full of people plotting against each other. This friend of my parents blew the whistle on what he reckoned was a cycle of violence and cover-ups by the staff at one of these borstals. This became national debate between those defending either side. I've looked over the press cuttings of the time and it's clear to me that both sides had very good reason to think that the other side had plotted against them. Each side would have imagined things about the other, made claims about the other, tried to figure out what the other side's 'real' motives were and so on. I have a recollection of my parent's friend telling one part of the story with excited indignation, the veins on his neck sticking out. I'm sure he believed he was right – but then I'm sure the 'other side' would have felt the same.

Of course, it could be that you are being conspired against. If you stick your head above the parapet, and particularly if you do some whistleblowing, there's every chance you will find yourself at the heart of real conspiracies. These may well merge with our imagined ones. In other words, just as the gag says, 'Just because I'm paranoid, it doesn't mean that they're not out to get me.' (See, it does have a use!) What's more, these national tales of paranoia, founded or unfounded, also become part of who we are. They are part of how we figure out the way the world works. When we see conspiracies unfolding in the news or in our favourite TV drama, it can lead us to conspiratorial thinking ourselves. And in instances like the borstal scandal, the difference between the two types of feeling is not so clear. It became blurred.

The best bit of blurred paranoia I know (we all have favourites) is Shakespeare's *Hamlet*. Hamlet is not only fearful and suspicious of everyone around him, but he also has very good reason to feel this way about most of them. Every time I see the play, I wonder about Hamlet's efforts to stay ahead of his paranoia while at the same time trying to stay ahead of real threats to his life. One method he tries out is to feign going crazy. Or, we wonder, is he really going crazy? Or, does he try so hard to feign going crazy that he becomes crazy anyway? And did he feign being crazy because really, there was no other option open to him?

I find such speculations when watching or reading these kinds of characters really helpful. This is the reading cure: bibliotherapy, as it's called. As we read, we put ourselves in the story. When we finish the book or film or play, we are left with scenes in our head. We select the ones that have particular power or relevance to ourselves. We don't necessarily do this consciously. It just happens. But then we can ask, why do I remember that particular moment? What is it about me that made that moment important for me?

At other times, the happenings in a small institution – an office, a school, a hospital or even a club or group – stay there. These can easily be as intense, if not more so, than the ones that are projected into a bigger environment. On several occasions people working in these environments have told me that they are victims of some kind of hate campaign or coup. Two friends of mine worked for the same organisation and started to become suspicious that they were being elbowed out. They put in front of me 'evidence': a long line of put-downs, jobs complained of, meetings cancelled, agreements broken, inexplicably big bust-ups over trivial things to do with emails not sent, and so it went on. I heard them out several times – together and separately. I could see that it was having a toll on them. They felt that they had sunk their heart and soul into the outfit, but that effort was now being disregarded.

My first thought was to focus on the hard, rational bit: who did this outfit actually belong to? I've since discovered that a lot of us work in places where our contracts, commitments or duties are not entirely clear. Maybe it could be a small enterprise that a group of friends set up. Of course, everyone was friends at the beginning! Then, for whatever reason, things became less harmonious or our various visions changed and the elbowing started. At that moment, the questions of who works for whom, who owns what – all those bubble to the surface. The boundaries begin to blur as anxieties grow. People who used to be family friends suddenly become thieving bastards – either in our minds, or really, or a mixture of both. Good old reliable chums become stab-in-the-back merchants. Even the most innocuous of comments become sly digs. In the end, in these situations the only way out is the way out. Cut your losses and leave with your dignity and sanity intact. I'm not suggesting it's easy, especially if you are leaving something that you have invested a lot of hope and love in. We see this played out with the break-up of bands.

Fifty years or more after the Beatles broke up, Paul McCartney is still mithering over how he and John Lennon became so bitter towards each other.

So my first response to those in this situation is a very dull one: what are your responsibilities? My second is: who are your friends? Paranoia can feed on loneliness. Ask yourself, do you have people close to you, people you can trust? Paranoia shrinks in the face of trust. If you can find someone you can trust, at work or in any other context, then this can often help you sort out in your mind what's real, what's unreal and what you can or can't do next. It's true in the workplace of course, but applies in many other settings too.

In the end, my friends cut and run. I've seen this repeated several times in my life. People make the decision that life is too short and living with a sense of persecution, paranoia, being underappreciated or plain just not wanted is too much. Sometimes there's a price to pay – quite literally, if you lose income – or it might be less clearly defined: you may lose creativity, or ownership, or the goodwill of clients. This can 'prove', in one's mind, that the motive of your former partners or colleagues was greed.

If you are embroiled in a situation like this, either as a victim or a sympathetic ear, you may want to bring the cold wind of reason to bear on the matter. Are the people who have wronged you, your friends, or greedy, selfish, heartless, scheming swine? Maybe there's some separating out that can be done. People are entitled to want to break out of an old set-up. What they're not entitled to do is to do it shiftily, dishonestly or in ways that deprive someone of what they're entitled to; but people do, even the best people. In these situations, the cut and run can be the best option. Sometimes, though, you may be able to separate the motive from the method, to make a distinction between what the 'enemy' intends to do – which might even be some-what understandable – from the way they're going about doing it. This can help you to move on, as can focussing on the practicalities of the next steps: the facts and figures. That is a great way to progress, and to get better. Getting these things sorted can be both a useful distraction from the paranoid stuff, and useful in themselves. Progress!

It goes without saying that there may well be an aftermath: bitterness. *How could my former best friends do this to me? I hope they bloody well fail now that I've gone. See, the stuff they do now is nowhere near as good as it was when I was working with them.* These feelings can easily mix with the old paranoias we had when we were still in that set-up. They are the other side of the same coin: feelings of suspicion, dislike, rivalry combined with egotism and narcissism.

The cliché that comes to mind is 'let it go'. Oh, how much more easily said than done! In fact, it's possible (a theory of mine, coming up) that in the end, in real life, it is actually impossible to let go entirely. Letting go has just become something we say to people to try to help them be less bothered by feeling fearful, hateful or vengeful towards others. Maybe we should think of something less simplistic than letting go? Something to do with admitting that in reality, we will keep hold of these memories and feelings but we have to find ways that stop them hurting or eating us up. Not so much a matter of letting go as 'altering our grip', just as we might do with something heavy in our hand that is hurting our fingers. We can't just let go of the shopping – we need the food in the bag. What we can do is alter our grip. If we go on and on holding the shopping in the same way, the handles bite into our fingers. That is, if we go on and on repeating the same feelings, the same sayings, the same scenes that arise in our paranoid minds, then they will bite into us. Can we find a way to alter our hold on them?

One way to do this is to do what all scriptwriters and novelists do: change the point of view. I'll explain: when we do these repeated run-throughs in our mind of the horrible things other people have done to us, we repeat the way we look at them. The pattern is always 'Aggrieved Me' looking at 'Horrible Them'. How can we change that? For one moment – no matter how unbearable – we can try putting ourselves in the shoes of Horrible Them. We can ask questions like: why might they have done what they did? How might they regard me? What do I look like through their eyes? What exactly is it that they were trying to do and why? In this bit of mind-work, you may find that you discover very important differences between the people who were really out to get you and others who weren't. You may find that you had contributed to why you were treated in the way you were. You may discover what the others' rights really are. On the other hand, you may of course find that all your worst suspicions are entirely confirmed! Either way, a shift in point of view can relieve your paranoia, especially where the paranoia involves your belief that people are bad doing things to you for not much more reason than because it's what they do.

I'm someone who is quite capable of sitting in an annoyed, imaginative state for some time after I feel I've experienced an injustice. The longer I sit in it, the wider it becomes. But I don't want to stay in that place. I don't want to feel like a victim. A way of lifting myself out of this is to put myself in the other's shoes, as I have explained, but sometimes, more is needed.

On those occasions, I have learned how to put up a shield. As I used to say in mock-boxing matches with my kids: 'Block!' This runs counter to a lot of modern thought about mediation and conciliation, which often suggest that the only way to move on is to negotiate and talk it through. That's 100 per cent appropriate where a situation has to be resolved, as with legal matters. However, sometimes we find ourselves in situations where there isn't something specific that has to be resolved, and we find that the talk is part of the problem and not part of the solution. I've been there.

If you feel that the talking hurts, then as a last resort we can 'Block!' We have to make ourselves impervious to what is wounding us. It might mean ending contact. It might mean only agreeing contact through someone else, the 'intermediary'. This, perhaps, is a tale of extreme measures – not to be applied in all, or even many, situations. It's just that sometimes, perhaps rarely, the only way to keep your inner self safe is to turn the volume off. When I've needed this, it's been a useful technique. And I did feel safe. It worked.

Chapter 8

Eddie

I'll start this chapter by telling you a story. I'm telling it to you so you know what happened. I'm also telling it to you because it helps me to tell it. And because it helps me, I am saying that if anything like this has happened to you, it may well help you to do the same: to tell your story. You can do this in any way you like. The important thing is to tell it.

The story begins at Paddington Station in 1999. From there, I ring home to see if my son Eddie is in. He's nearly 19 and sometimes he's there and sometimes he stays with his girlfriend. If he's not there, I might go and visit someone else. If he is there, I'll go home and we can have a chat or maybe play *FIFA* – the football video game.

It turns out that he is at home. He's not feeling too

good, he says. A bit of a headache. I tell him to take some paracetamol and I'll be home in about an hour. I get on the tube and, sure enough, I'm home in about an hour.

He doesn't seem too bad. Must be one of those things my mother used to call a 'chill' or a 'fluey thing', I think. I tell him that I've worked a thing into my show for children where I tell them a story about when he was a funny, naughty toddler, then, I say, I follow it with a story about how he grew and grew and grew until, as he is now, he became bigger than me. And something else: now he can pick me up and whirl me round and round until I shout, 'Put me down, Eddie! Put me down, Eddie!' It works. To little children, as I mime the contrast between chasing after the naughty little toddler Eddie and being swung through the air by the giant Eddie, it seems miraculous that one day they could be bigger than me. I think it's a miracle too. Eddie seems to enjoy the story.

He doesn't go to bed. We sit in the living room, have something to eat, watch TV. He's written a play and we talk about how we could get some people together to do a kind of acted-out reading. I'll get in touch with someone I know, I say, someone who works with young actors.

He has a pager (remember them?) and pages his girlfriend. He stretches out on the sofa – he really is bigger than me – says that he feels a bit weird. I feel his head. It's hot. I remind him that he can alternate between paracetamol and ibuprofen and line up the boxes for him, warning him not to overdo the dose.

He says he's going to bed now, but he'll have some ice cream first. He says he's hot. I ask him if his neck is stiff. It's something I've done with the children for the previous few years since meningitis has come up on the radar. I remember that I took his sister to A & E not that long before when she had a high temperature, stiff neck and felt sick. She was clear. No, he says, he doesn't have a stiff neck.

Someone's sent me a book of riddles that's just come out. I've got it because a riddle I've written is in the book. I read it to him. He gets it. It's daft. The answer, he says, is 'your bum'.

Those are the last words that I ever heard him say.

He goes out of the room.

I hear him go to the kitchen to get some ice cream and then I hear him on the stairs.

When I go to bed, I put my head round the door. He's lying on his back in bed.

'You OK?' I ask.

He nods without making a sound. I check that he's got the paracetamol, ibuprofen and a glass of water by his bed and then I go to my room and turn in.

In the night, I hear him get up and go to the loo. I have a feeling of irritation that I'm awake. I've got to get up early and I don't want to feel tired. I fall back asleep.

I've got to get on the road pretty early so I'm up at six. I pop my head round the door to check how he's been in the night.

'I've got to go, Edz,' I say. 'I know it's early.' I think I'll remind him to double-lock the door on his way out.

He doesn't answer.

I feel his head. It's cold. He's still. Unnervingly still. I nudge him. He feels like a rock. There's no movement, no life. I know – but don't know – that he's dead. I shake him, shouting out to him, 'Eddie! Eddie!' There's no reply. I rush to get the phone, ring 999, ask for 'Ambulance'. I describe what's happened.

'Pull him out of the bed,' the voice says, 'pull him on to the floor, lie him on his side.'

I grab hold of him, and do what I'm told. It's hard. He weighs more than me. As I pull him, I see that his arm is stiff, at an angle, as if it's in a plaster without any plaster on it. His armpit has strange red stripes. I get him on to the floor, and when I lie him on his side, a bit of pale red fluid comes out of his mouth on to the carpet.

I get back on the phone, I tell them what I've done and what I've seen.

The voice says, 'We'll be there in a few minutes.'

I'm alone with Eddie in the room. I think he's

dead. I know he's dead. I think that the ambulance people will come and they'll do something that will make him come alive.

I don't remember the next few minutes. At some point, I notice that there's a splurge of ice cream in the loo. I think how when he got up in the night he must have vomited it up. I don't know now what I thought or did before the ambulance came. I remember at one point thinking or saying, 'Why have you done this, Eddie?' as if he had done this thing to me. I'm almost ashamed to admit it, though. Why or how could I have thought at that moment that I was in any way involved in him getting whatever it was that had killed him? Well, I guess it's part of how we see the death of those we love: we see them withdrawing their love from us and if ever, in our past, people withdrew their love from us as some kind of punishment, then someone dying can feel like that too.

The ambulance people call, I let them in, they dash upstairs, their bulky uniforms filling the space. They kneel over Eddie, and in a few seconds, one of them says, 'He's dead.'

In the next few seconds they ask me for his date of birth, if he took drugs, if he was drunk. They call the police and a doctor – was it one of our doctor friends who lived on our street? There were three of them. Three doctors within a hundred yards of the house. I'm not sure.

There are whispers between the ambulance people, the doctor and the police.

In the meantime, I realise I have to call his mother, his girlfriend, his brothers and sisters, my father and stepmother.

I hear myself saying the impossible, 'Eddie has died.' I don't remember all their reactions. I guess that's because I can't bear to remember them. I'm afraid of remembering them. I do remember that his girlfriend thought I was joking. Fair enough, we had each developed the art of crazy phone calls, doing voices, trying to trick each other into believing crazy stuff. One of his sisters asked me plaintively why hadn't I taken him to the hospital. I mutter something about him not having a stiff neck.

I start to feel deeply, hopelessly, helplessly guilty. I have failed utterly and completely. It's my fault that he's died. By not saving him, I have killed him.

Sooner than I know, the street is full of people, the front door is open and people are rushing in and out. Eddie's mother, his girlfriend and his brothers and sisters start coming over.

People are in the kitchen making tea, coming over with food, cooking, sitting silently looking at the floor, whispering to each other.

The ambulance people tell me that they're going to take Eddie away. They put him in a bag. I hear the zip. They get ready to pick him up to take him out of the house but he's too heavy so they slide the bag down the stairs. I watch it glide over the steps, I hear the sound of it bumping down. Then he's gone.

It emerges that what's killed him is meningitis, or to be more precise, meningococcal septicaemia. I think of the posters I've seen at the GP surgery. Headache, fever, stiff neck, sickness, rash – do the test to see if the rash stays even when you press it with a glass. He had no rash, I say to myself. I didn't see a rash. He didn't see a rash.

We try to comfort each other, more people fill the house, turning up with more food and cards. They sit and talk.

There's a row. Is someone trying to start an argument with me? I am bewildered that this is happening, even at this moment, less than a few hours after Eddie has died. I feel myself smile inside. I remember a line from somewhere about fate laughing at us.

The house stayed full for days and days. People kept coming and going. I felt I was being carried by them. They weren't going to let go of me. They were keeping an eye on me. Eddie's mother said that he couldn't and shouldn't be in the morgue. She couldn't bear the idea of him being somewhere all alone in such a cold place. So we asked for him to be brought back, laid out in an open coffin in the living room.

People brought flowers. He was surrounded by flowers. The room was heavy with the smell of them. People went in one by one, in pairs and groups to see him. I watched my father saying to Eddie's younger brother, 'I'll take you in', and they went in, just the pair of them to see him.

I stood by the coffin again and again. Sometimes I stroked his head and felt his hair. His face was dark.

One of the doctors from the street explained what happened. Meningitis is a bacterium that lives in our throats. One way or another most of us at some time or another have it in there. For some reason, not fully understood yet, the bacterium might migrate. It might inflame the membranes in our brain, which are called 'meninges'. Other times it might also migrate through the membranes in our throat into the blood. It thrives and multiplies in the blood and produces something that breaks down the walls of the blood cells and blood vessels. 'Basically,' the doctor said, 'your insides turn to mush.'

I remember that phrase over and over again. 'Your insides turn to mush.' He went on, 'If it's any comfort, he wouldn't have known a thing. He would have gone to sleep and known nothing more.'

I think again and again about being Eddie, his thoughts as he dozed and went into sleep. Was he calm? What did he think when he got up, went to the loo and vomited up the ice cream? Did he wonder if he should wake me up and tell me that he felt lousy? How bad did he feel?

And then the unbearable to think about, he went back to bed and some time in the early hours of the morning faded away, his innards turning to mush.

I noticed, when he was laid out at home, that he was growing white fur round his hairline. Tiny little white hairs were growing at the very top of his forehead.

I dreaded going to bed because I knew that I would have to wake up in the morning and discover again that he had died. I decided to pretend that he was alive. It's just that he isn't here. Like when he stayed at his girlfriend's place. It was easy. It worked. Then as the day unfolded I'd let myself gently acknowledge that he had died. But 'died'? What did that mean? Just that he wasn't here. But he was 'out there' somewhere, surely?

One of the doctors explained that the hairs weren't growing. His body was shrinking, and the hairs were protruding through the skin.

My old friends Jeff and Carol came to see us. Not all that long before, they had lost their only son in a road accident. I remembered Jeff talking to me about how it took him to the deepest point of despair, wondering what it's all for. They told us stories of how they did what they could to remember their son. How some days all they could do was go into a wood and howl. Jeff is brilliant with his hands – painting, sculpting, print-making, film-making. They told me how he had carved an old tree trunk. I thought of how big and physical that was. How you could put all your anger and grief into hammering a chisel into a bit of timber. I wondered what I would do that could be so total. They seemed so brave and full of hope. I wondered if I could ever reach that point too.

I remember people telling me that they made a life book of the child they lost. *Maybe I'll make a life book*, I thought.

I talked to my father's friend, Wayne, in the US. Phyllis and he and their lovely family had lost Richard. About the same age as Eddie. It had all happened decades ago. What did they know about how to go on living? Wayne talked slowly and carefully. Told me how people are good to you. Apart from one. Apart from one? I said. There'll be someone who'll say the wrong thing. 'What did they say to you?' I said. 'She said, "Well, at least you've got other children,"' Wayne told me. 'You just have to push it away. Don't let it get to you,' he said.

Then we planned the funeral. We thought of all the people who would like to speak, all the people we would like to have there, all the bits of music we wanted. He had friends I hardly knew: friends from school, friends from the theatres he had been working in as a 'crew man', part of the team of people who move the props, sets and curtains for a theatre show. I remembered some of them. He had been working at the big West End theatres: the Apollo, the Lyric. He told me how he used to bring on the helicopter in *Miss Saigon* or press the button to make a giant lectern rise up in a Ben Elton play. One night he couldn't do the job, and he couldn't find anyone to 'dep' for him, so he asked me if I could do it. Sure I could. So one night I made my way to the Apollo, signed in for him, pressed the button for a giant lectern to rise up. 'When you get paid,' one of the crew said, 'keep the money. We're not having it that he gets a dep who gives him the wages.' (It was banter, of course.) I remembered one of them coming over to watch a Mike Tyson fight on the TV. They would all have to come to the funeral . . . more and more people kept coming into my mind . . . the hockey guys . . . of course, for several years, he had been 'Big Eddie' who played in goal for the Arsenal Community Sports junior hockey team run by the wonderful Freddie.

The funeral was lovely. Is that a strange thing to say? Not a bit of it. As I knew from my mother's, a funeral that causes you to be irritated or angry or more sad than you would be anyway, has to be avoided. A funeral must live in your mind as a good moment. We tried to make sure that the funeral worked for all of us. A friend from the BBC made a montage of commentaries from Arsenal's recent successes, games that Eddie and I had been to together. The poet James Berry read the poem my father had written for the day, about Eddie, 'larger than life, but not large enough'. I've included that poem at the end of this chapter. Eddie had also struck up a friendship with an old Jewish friend of mine, someone who was exploring just how far he wanted to take his interests in Judaism, Hebrew and Yiddish. He said the Kaddish for him.

I could go on, but this is a book about getting better. How do you get better from something as total and as devastating as this? If I can magnify the pain once more, I'll say this: Eddie had become one of those people in a family who is a pivot. There are different parts to a 'blended' family or 'network' family (siblings with different mothers or fathers), so one sibling might not link up with another part very closely. There may be ways in which one sibling chafes against another. Eddie had stood at some centre point where all the siblings pivoted around him. He was the one person equally beloved of all of them. He could sit on the sofa between two who were angry with each other and they would each be happy to snuggle up with him and joke with him. I had thought it was magical. I didn't know how he did it. I cherished it more than anything else in the world. And now there was a hole. There was a gap on the sofa. How would I cope with it?

What follows is not a menu. It's not a prescription. I know better than many that being told how to mourn is one of the most irritating things in the world. We each have to find our own ways of doing it. We can watch what others do, listen to what people say, but in the end we have to make it work for whoever we are and whatever life situation we're in. And there's another thing: by making it your own, you have the sense that it's you doing it, you're the 'agent'. You can take pride in your own ability to do something in the face of the impossible. Just following someone else's plan won't do that for you.

So I offer you what I did as a set of things to think about, ignore, adapt, change, or do what you want with. I hope they give you ideas for what you might want to do if you're faced with loss or grief. Just that.

I spent a long time finding out about meningitis. I was desperate that this 'thing' shouldn't sit in my mind like a mysterious phantom that had appeared in the night and sucked the lifeblood out of my son. I'm a huge fan of the kind of fiction that gives us images like that. That's because, for me, they have what is called 'psychic reality', where our feelings are real even as we look at an image that we don't believe in: like Edvard Munch's *The Scream*. No one really looks like that person in the painting but it's a picture of a feeling we can recognise. We may feel like that person too. But when faced with Eddie's death, I decided I didn't need a phantom – I wanted to know all that doctors know.

How did that help? It put what had happened into the context of the human race. It showed that Eddie's death wasn't just or only something that had happened to me, to his family, to his friends. It was something that happened to the human race and was part of the human story. We live with bacteria. Bacteria live with us. This is how it's been for millions of years. We evolve with each other. The death of Eddie was a moment when the bacterium was so successful it failed: it killed its host and then died with it. To know these things helped me, and still does. It's the only way I can make sense of it. Any other way feels to me senseless. I don't believe in a fate or destiny that governs us. I don't believe that it's the will of a being outside of life on earth. I don't even think any kind of 'will' comes into it. It's biology.

I also wanted to know about other people who had died of meningitis. That's because I didn't want to feel alone with this thing. And I wanted to know how people were coping with losing someone in this way. Who? Where? When? How? The internet had just got going. In fact, the computer I had was entirely down to Eddie. He had helped me choose it, set it up and had played games on it. Now I searched and made contact with others who had lost loved ones with meningitis. I particularly wanted to know of nearly-19-year-olds. I wanted to know that I wasn't unique in having missed that it was meningococcal septicaemia. I felt lonelier than I had ever felt before when I thought of myself going into his room and finding him dead or if I thought of myself as the only person in the world who had done that. That's a nearly unbearable thing to feel. I found out, of course, that I wasn't alone in that experience either.

I started to learn a lot of things: in some US states, those stripes that I spotted in his armpit had been added to the list of things to look out for – rashes in the armpits and groin. Sometimes, it's the first place they appear. I tried to get the NHS to add this to their posters. I didn't manage to win that one, but I did find myself talking to the meningitis charities. We talked about whether anyone was researching whether this or that genetic make-up or life-story pre-disposed a person to getting meningitis. I was wondering what was it about Eddie that caused the bacterium in him, on that day, at that time, to get through the membranes in his throat. I ran through his life, like a rapid film montage remembering the illnesses he'd had, the allergies, the lifestyle, the stresses and strains. It was a way of telling the story of his life to myself. I did it then and have done it a thousand times since, in many different ways. In a way, I was trying to find out the natural history of the meningitis bacterium, just as we might learn about the natural history of dandelions or bison: what habitats do they like? What can they cope with? What can't they cope with? What predisposes them to thrive or weaken?

Around this time, I was interviewed by newspapers and radio about how Eddie died. The first one on radio became political. A very kind, thoughtful interviewer, the husband of a colleague who had 'produced' me on radio, asked me questions. On one of those first raw days after he died, I told him how I had been. Following on after me, the then chief medical officer was asked about meningitis vaccinations. There was one available for two of the strains (not all). Why weren't all children being vaccinated with it? my friend asked him. The CMO wasn't happy. Stats about how 300-plus people died of it every year circulated in the broadcast. There was a moment's chat about whether that was many or a few. At the end, the rather grumpy CMO warned my interviewer, the BBC and the public that he wasn't going to be 'bumped' into bringing in a mass meningitis vaccination programme.

As I listened, I wondered if I was going to become one of those people who crusade for a cause related to the reason why their child died. *Why not?* I thought. I could campaign for the vaccine, just as the meningitis charities were doing at that very moment. I've met people who find campaigning like that a great help.

They say that it helps them to think that their loved one didn't die in vain. Some good will come of it. But there was no need to campaign for the vaccine. A few months later, the CMO announced that they were going to introduce the meningitis vaccine for all new-borns. I sometimes comfort myself that that awkward, tetchy interview may have contributed in one small way to a change of heart at the ministry. I have no idea if it did. It's just something that I like to tell myself. A bit of self-delusion goes a long way some-times. Grab what you can.

More personally, Eddie's mother and I decided to go to Paris. I'm not sure how or why that idea evolved. Perhaps it was the kind offer of one of my oldest friends, François, who I first met when I was a teen-ager. It seemed to make sense to talk to each other away from other people, in a place that was full of sights and smells that we both liked. There was no way that we were going to start up a relationship again. It wasn't like that. For me, it was to do with trust and solidarity in the face of the fact that we both adored Eddie and were now utterly bereft. François had just taken on a flat in Montparnasse, it was empty, newly painted and polished. All it had was a table, chairs and a couple of beds. It was hollow and echoey. The lights from the street decorated the walls.

In the daytime, we walked about randomly look-ing at street markets, buildings, the river. We weren't revisiting a place we had shared. If anything, it was new. I have no idea why all this felt soothing to me but it did. One time, we walked past the entrance to the Montparnasse cemetery. Neither of us knew at that moment what kind of cemetery it is but on a whim, we decided to walk in. In fact, it's one of Paris's two huge secular cemeteries, full of monuments to some of France's most famous people – or indeed, people from other countries who've died in France. Walking about amongst them was a strange relief. I think it made me think of Eddie as gone and now in some way in the company of the dead. I don't believe in the afterlife, so what I mean is that just as there were monuments and stones there, with people visiting them, so I was already beginning to make monuments and inscriptions in my head. Not real ones. Not even blueprints for one that we might make. The imagined place in my head, the place that was Eddie, was like one of the tombstones in the cemetery. Because we had no guide or plan, we randomly and pleasingly 'met' the historic figures there, people we knew from our studies or interests: the poet Charles Baudelaire; the feminist writer Simone de Beauvoir; the singer Serge Gainsbourg, whose stone was littered with cigarettes in a kind of tribute; Guy de Maupassant, whose stories I had read in my French class; the surrealist couple Juliet and Man Ray, whose inscription was: 'Unconcerned but not indifferent'. What did that mean?; and hundreds more. This may sound strange, but it felt friendly. The word 'companionable' came to mind. I felt like I was in good 'company'.

At one point, by a high wall, we came across a woman crying. There were flowers and photos on the grave. We stood with her. She spoke to me. She said that the grave was for her son but I noticed that she could hardly speak through her crying. I said that we had just lost our son too. I told her it was an illness. She said that her son died in an accident. When? I asked her. Ten years before, she said.

A wave of feeling came over me. The moment she said that, I felt a mix of sorrow and fright. It was desperately sad that this woman was so consumed by grief, but it frightened me that she was this sad so long after the event. I then thought something that may seem heartless. I said to myself – I most certainly didn't say it out loud – 'I don't want to be like her in ten years' time.' To tell the truth, I was afraid that I would be. I felt like her in that very moment, my mind full of Eddie, thinking every minute about not having him there, and knowing that I would never have him there again. I felt like this woman sounded. But would I feel like that in a year's time? Ten years' time? I hoped not.

I wished the poor woman well and walked on.

We went into knick-knack shops and bookshops

and various Parisian tourist traps. I guess that in our separate ways we were looking for mementos, things that we could keep that would commemorate Eddie and even, perhaps, commemorate our efforts to cope. I bought a plate. And then I was in a poster and print shop and saw a postcard. It was a reproduction of an eighteenth-century print illustration of a fable. It showed a man carrying an elephant. I looked at it and it was me. *I am a man carrying an elephant*, I thought. Because the print is of that period, it is beautifully engraved, very realistic. It looked as if the man really was staggering up a mountain path with an elephant on his back. I bought the postcard. Later, I wrote about it and called my book of poems about Eddie dying *Carrying the Elephant*.

A picture, a song, a snatch of music, a line of a poem, play or story can chime with us. It's in tune with our feelings in the moment. That postcard seemed like a lifeline to me in my grief. I could reach out and grab it and it had the power to see me through this time. It said what I wanted to say, gave words and image to how I felt. It's an absurd metaphor. Of course, a man can't carry an elephant up a mountain. But the extreme absurdity helped express how extreme I felt. Thank you to that eighteenth-century artist, Jean-Baptiste Oudry.

Talking of music though – in the early days after he died, I couldn't bear to listen to any. I started to think that music was cruel. The shortest of sequences of notes could send me into a well of misery. What was the point? Even worse was any song that had a link to Eddie. He once told me that his girlfriend was a huge fan of the band R.E.M., in particular of the lead singer, Michael Stipe. He wanted me to lend him some money to buy him and her tickets to go and see them. I didn't know their stuff, but not long after Eddie died, I was watching TV and saw them do 'Everybody Hurts'. I felt the bitter irony that his girl-friend loved their songs so much and, I guessed, must have known and loved this song too. I didn't dare talk to her about it though. For at least a year or two I did what I could to avoid hearing it.

Back home, we did what we could to look after each other. It wasn't easy. I thought it was all the harder because this 'network' family was spread out – we came and went, met up, disappeared, came back again. We each did things to commemorate Eddie, sometimes on our own, sometimes together, some-times with others who knew him in the different worlds he lived in. I've always loved these, loved each time I see people being kind, enjoying something about Eddie, remembering the things he said and did. To me, they feel like happy, strong occasions.

One of them is organised by the hockey team that he played for. I loved watching his games – Eddie used to stand like a giant in the little hockey goal, padded up in the huge pads that hockey goalies wear, and over the top he wore various garish 'gridiron' shirts that I bought him on my trips to the US. Every year since he died, his old team gather together for a game. It's more than 20 years now, so those lads have grown up – some of them have had children, got a bit paunchy, taken on responsibilities in schools, firms, offices, councils and the like. People who didn't know him join in, and the children too. Life goes on.

Before the game starts, we have a 30-second silence for him. The game is full of banter and antics. We all hope that Darren can manage a cartwheel, they beg me to come on and pretend I can play (I can't). I bring my son, the one who was born after Eddie died, and to everyone's delight, he whizzes about like a pro. At the end, we have speeches. At the core of this whole event is Freddie, head of community sports at Arsenal. He trained and nurtured that team, working with hundreds of young people in the borough. He is wise and kind beyond words, gently helping and nudging the youngsters through physical exercise, helping people find confidence and achievement. You couldn't think of anyone less like the stereotype of the barking sports coach, ripping people apart if he thinks they aren't good enough. I know Eddie loved him and in turn Freddie gave Eddie space to be the team clown and recycler of jokes that even I wasn't allowed to hear.

After the speeches, the award. One of the lads made a little wooden plinth. Mounted on the plinth is a goalkeeper's glove. In the palm of the glove is a bottle of beer. It's a witty, loving reminder of why and how they remember Eddie. It's always my job to hand it over to whoever has played the best that day. I choose. It's often Darren, so long as he managed the cartwheel. I know that Darren and Eddie had a strong friendship. I remember that when Eddie died, Darren came to see me and was too overwhelmed to speak.

As I look at them all, of course I think of what Eddie might have done, what he might have become. Maybe a writer. That play he wrote that I was going to help him put on? We did put it on – thanks to the theatre director, Sonia Ritter, we did a rehearsed reading. Then, thanks to a very old friend, *Good Morning?* was put on at the Edinburgh Festival.

In his programme notes, the producer Robert Silman wrote:

> *Eddie was enamoured of theatre and had just sent me the script of his first play,* Good Morning? *I thought it was tremendous, not just a talented first play by a young author, but a tour de force. I wasn't able to tell Eddie how much I enjoyed his play, so this production is my opportunity to make amends.*

> *The production went on to play to sold-out audiences, and*

was named one of the top five current productions nationwide by The Times. It had some other great reviews too, like this from The Stage:

> *A wickedly funny farce . . . Eddie Rosen has left an absolute gift to his actors . . . their characters are unnervingly real . . . a wonderfully simple concept even funnier for continually threatening to slip into deliciously darker territory . . . Put this on in the West End and you'll easily attract a whole new generation of theatregoers.*

This is both beautiful and painful. It's very hard to take, thinking about the things that might have been, that could have been. I have to try hard (and it is an effort) to accept what he did, he did, and that's it. We each have a lifespan. His lifespan was nearly 19 years. That was his run. That's all that his mind and body could take, given its encounters with the dangers, viruses and bacteria that are around us all the time. We can only do what we can do in the time that we end up with.

For a few years, his old school put on a poetry festival in Eddie's name. People showered me with cards and presents. Outside in the garden, there is an olive tree that my old friend and agent Charles gave me in honour of Eddie. It's survived some hard winters and dry summers. I love that it has. Every year, Eddie's brothers and sisters, their partners and children, his mother, me and my newer family all meet up on the day he died.

What about ashes, a stone? We divvied the ashes up. One of Eddie's sisters took her portion to the edge of a cliff in Cornwall and at the moment of the eclipse of the sun, threw the ashes towards the sea. No one said it, but maybe we all thought it: an eclipse seemed to fit how we felt. Something had been eclipsed. That was a holiday I look back on as balm. People more kind than I can say, Jeff and Jude and their children, took us, looked after us, and we played cricket on the sand, dabbled about in canoes, caught mackerel and cooked them on the beach. No one asked me to explain anything, talk about anything. No one told me what to think or how to grieve. It was a time of acceptance and daftness. It sits in the gallery of good things in my mind. It's nice to gather these up, cherish them. They remind me that some people just know what are the right things to do.

Some ashes sat about in people's houses for a while, before my wife Emma suggested that we could have a grave. In a lovely cooperative venture, we found a plot in Highgate Cemetery, sought out a hulky, rough stone and discussed what to engrave on it. We agreed on a phrase from my father's poem – 'Larger than life' – along with his full name and dates. We met up in the rain for a little family ceremony. Ashes were poured in below the stone, and there it sits, not far from the writers George Eliot (Mary Evans by birth) and Douglas Adams, and not all that far from Karl Marx. So far, I haven't gone to see it again. I ask myself why not?, and for the time being, I don't have an answer.

But what about writing? For more than a year, I hardly wrote a thing. Every time I tried, it all felt too big. There was too much of it. There were too many details. Too much story. No place to start. Then, one day, Emma and I were reading some poems by the American writer Raymond Carver. One of them is called 'Locking Yourself Out, Then Trying to Get Back In'. It tells the story of how Carver (or someone) locks himself out of his study but then looks into the room where he works. It's written almost as if he was talking it on to the page, and it slowly gathers force as it moves from the details of what he is doing and what he can see, into his thoughts about his life. I was overwhelmed by it. I thought of Eddie's empty room. I hadn't touched it. Carver's poem seemed to be about him thinking of what his room would look like after he died, and in a way I had done that with Eddie's room. Eddie's room was the future that Carver had seen.

Reading the poem over and over handed me what felt like an invite: 'You can write like this, Michael.' I often think that one person's writing can offer us a possibility. It can say without saying it, 'You can write like this, if you want to.' Carver's poem did that for me. 'You can sit down with a bit of paper and talk calmly and drily in the Carver way about what you've seen and heard, what you've done and every now and then – not too much! – say what you think. But don't get too dressy! Don't fill it up with too much emotion. Let the reader figure that out from the pictures and sounds you give them.' Carver didn't tell me that. I didn't ever meet him. I took that from his poem.

From that moment, I found I could write. I found what I call a corridor between how I felt in that moment and other things that had happened in my life. I wrote them out in fragments, some shorter than Carver's, some about the same length. I wasn't too fussed about writing in a way removed from how I speak. I like how writing conversationally feels to me as I write and read it back to myself. It makes me feel as if I'm there. I wrote down dreams, memories, conversations, thoughts. As I mentioned, these became the book *Carrying the Elephant*. And as with everything else in this chapter, I am offering you a possibility. You may read a poem or a story. If you get the feeling at any point as you read that you could write something that is a bit like the passage you're reading, seize the time, just do it. Just scribble it down. If you like the sound of the Carver-Rosen method (!) that I've just described, just do it. A little note or two in an exercise book to get you going. You don't need to show it to anyone, you're doing this for you. I found it to be a huge help. I'll talk more about it in the next chapter.

Then, one day, in 2002, I was doing my family show at the Edinburgh Festival. Every year, I've tried to do at least one show at the Children's Book Festival that goes on in marquees in the middle of Charlotte Square. I had eliminated my Eddie stories from my act. I was afraid of doing them, in case I broke down. So I did my poems, my ad libs, my stories – it's like stand-up for children or anyone who wants to come. At the end, I try to leave time for questions. One child had a question for me: 'What's Eddie doing now?' She had read my book, *Quick, Let's Get Out of Here*, which had what children sometimes called the 'Eddie Stories' in it. They're tales of him as a rumbustious toddler that had begun as ad libs on my school visits and ended up as free-verse poems. Now, here was a girl who had read those and worked out that Eddie would be perhaps 20 or so by now. So what was he doing? What funny stories might I be able to tell about him now? I said, 'Eddie died. He caught an illness called meningitis and died.' The marquee was packed. It had been full of laughter and giggles. Now it went silent. For some, it was the first time they had heard what had happened to Eddie. For those who knew, it was what I call an 'elbow moment' – when things are going along in one direction, take someone's elbow and go off in another. The girl nodded. There were more hands up. I chose another child. He asked me what was my favourite poem when I was a child.

It was as if the water closed over the question about Eddie. It was gone. It was part of the way we were, chatting away. There were questions about favourite poems (or favourite colours, or about how Quentin Blake does his drawings), then came a question that had an answer to do with the death of my son, and then more questions about my favourite football team, or who inspired me to write. I thought about this afterwards. There was something strangely normal about what had happened. Eddie's death had slotted in alongside my other stuff. It was part of the flow of my life. A child had asked me about it and I had found a way in that moment of saying what had happened. I just said it, in my own words.

So, like the Raymond Carver poem, I had found a voice: a way of talking to a child about what happened to Eddie, or rather, to a family audience. When I had a moment, I put an imaginary child into my head – like the girl who had asked me that question – and told that imaginary child how I felt and what had happened. And I put that on to the page. As I did so, I felt very clear-headed. Even more than writing the poems for *Carrying the Elephant*, this felt like I was quietly and straightforwardly unloading stuff out of my mind. Maybe I had a pile of sand in the back of

173

my lorry, and I was digging it out and emptying my spade on to the ground.

This became my *Sad Book*, and it was a huge relief to write it. I then had the great good fortune of Quentin Blake being happy to do the art for it. He gave shape and rhythm and beauty to what I thought was a very plain tale of how I felt. He got to the very heart of what I felt and laid it out on page after page. Something odd: I hardly ever draw – apart from odd or funny flat cartoon faces and abstract doodles of buildings. When I wrote my *Sad Book*, I wrote it down in one of those reporter's notebooks, the ones where the pages are held at the top by little metal rings and you flip each page over the top. On the first page, I scribbled a picture of me grinning and I wrote, 'This is a picture of me feeling sad.' It was a simple cartoon and caption, a method of communicating ideas, thoughts, feelings and stories that goes back hundreds of years. There are examples on the walls of buildings that were engulfed by the volcano lava at Pompeii. All we need to do is try it. Again, it was something that helped me the moment I did it.

There is a satisfaction in doing something with your hands that expresses how you feel in your head. The satisfaction seems to come from doing it in a way that you think is right, that has grabbed your feelings so that you can read it back and say to yourself, 'Got it!' Even just that sense that you've done something good can be a moment of pleasure in the midst of all that grief.

As I write this, it's more than twenty years since Eddie died. Some of the clichés about death and loss are truths. When people say that bereavement moves from denial to anger to acceptance, it may sound glib but very grudgingly, I've come to agree. I hated hearing about those stages in the early days. You may hate hearing them now, but they have a ring of truth about them. I might complicate them, though, by saying that those three phases aren't really phases. There are overlaps and backtracks and there are times that one of those feelings – let's say it's the anger – erupts into the midst of the acceptance. I run with it.

Another saying is 'it's time to move on'. This annoyed me even more. My first feelings were that I didn't want to move on, I wanted to hang on to everything I could. How could I move on from something so precious? Why should I? Also, to consciously try to move on felt like a betrayal, as if I was rejecting Eddie, telling him that he didn't matter anymore. My dreams of him were – and still are – very vivid. He talks to me, he tells me things, he plays tricks on me, sometimes he tells me that he knows he's going to die. I can wake up and feel that he is watching me. If I 'move on', it can feel as if I am pushing him away. And yet, there are quite simply other things to do and things to feel other than sorrow. Without forcing it, we can make ourselves open to accepting opportunities and making space for feelings other than sadness. It's a question not so much of 'moving on' as 'letting things move'.

One of the ancient Greeks, Heraclitus, said, 'all is change'. Even if we do all we can to stand still, the world around us changes. People, buildings, countryside, weather – it's all changing all the time. There comes a point where you can ask yourself whether you want to change too, or not. I'll be honest, I find change hard. I'm a clinger. I love clinging on to my memories and old stuff. I have to push myself to try new things or accept new ways of being. But I do push myself. And it's been a huge help for me to think this way about change when I think about Eddie. He was a wonderful companion in that part of my life. He was on the road with me for nearly 19 years. But then he had to leave.

Before I end this chapter, I have to add something. Anyone who knows me would say that I've missed out something huge. Any account of me trying to deal with Eddie dying must surely include what happened in my life that was nothing to do with him: new beginnings, huge changes. And I must also understand that not everyone – far from it – who is bereaved can or will be able to imitate this bit of the story. I met Emma. We got married. We've had two children.

I've put into three short sentences as big a set of changes as anyone goes through by choice. There would be nothing more absurd or offensive of me to say to someone who's lost a loved one than, 'Get married! Have some kids!' It's just that if I want to be honest (and I do), then my story of coping with the death of Eddie can't be told without saying that the events of those three short sentences have probably contributed more than anything else to me having been able to cope, thrive and enjoy life. To love and to care for others and to be loved and cared for by others is immeasurably precious. I realise full well that I'm not saying anything new or helpful here. I'm just saying it so that you know that I do really understand that bereavement is, at the outset, hell, and that I know that getting to a point where it's not hell can take in some or any of the things I've talked about in this chapter. Yet, for me personally, I don't want to pretend that I got to where I've got to without the glorious times that I've expressed in those three short sentences.

You may be curious, then, am I like the Montparnasse woman in the cemetery? I have to say, no, I am not. I think about Eddie most days. He comes to me in my dreams quite often and waking up from them is not good. I avoid looking at photos of him – that almost feels too real. He's there, he's in me, he's around me. I talk about him. I repeat some of his jokes and favourite sayings. I retell the tricks he played on me, I even tell the 'Eddie stories' again, particularly when children in schools ask me to tell them. What am I, then? At ease with him? Is he 'at rest' in me and with me? Yes, I think it's something like that.

GRANDSON EDDIE,
BY MY FATHER, HAROLD ROSEN

Larger than life
Filling the frame of the doorway
In his hockey goalkeeper's gear
A giant from outer space

Larger than life.
Eddie in his Arsenal shirt
Acres of it across his chest
Stroking it with his great hands.

Eddie with his first watch
In the Natural History Museum
Checking the time every minute

GETTING BETTER

In charge of the rendez-vous
By the dinosaur
Making sure there is still some time left.

Nowhere near enough time
We now know.
Larger than life
But not large enough.

Chapter 9

One, two three – let's go!

I have to begin this chapter the same way I ended the last: with the help and love of my wife and children, and my love for them. I hope I help them too!

I can't talk about getting better without putting them in the picture. The problem is that when we think of the things we do to get better, we often leave our loved ones out. They become background noise. But a better analogy than background noise would be that they are the air we breathe. They are there supporting us, making it possible for us to do the things we do. I'm very aware that if I had been trying to handle Covid alone, or grief, or any other of the challenges I've faced, as some people have to, it would have been a massively harder task. Perhaps, given the person I am, impossible. Their support, along with the agency I've found in different coping strategies, has helped me in the long process of getting better.

As I've stressed in this book, it's important to find the ways (big or small) that you can feel in control of at least some of what is happening to you. This was really brought home to me in the aftermath of having Covid.

In June 2020, I was taken from St Pancras Rehabilitation Hospital to our home. I very carefully and proudly walked from the ambulance, across the pavement, up our path and in through the door. It was just about the longest walk without a stick that I had done so far.

My family had put out bunting for me: it said 'Welcome'. I was welcome, and I was home. But in other ways, the statement seemed strange: surely I hadn't been gone for very long? I knew I had been ill. I knew I had been in hospital. I knew that I had had to learn how to walk again. But the night when Emma and our daughter took me to A & E wasn't all that long ago, was it? Or was it?

It had in fact been three months, but I hadn't quite 'got' that yet. I couldn't compute it. I couldn't match how I felt right at that moment to the raw facts of the dates. So I didn't know it and didn't believe it. The reason for this, I know now, is that I had spent around 40 days 'heavily sedated' or 'in an induced coma', as they say. Being 'ventilated' didn't just mean having a mask over my face, it meant I had been knocked out. I still didn't fully understand what had happened to me in hospital. There was a lot of confusion for me, and confusion is worrying. Confusion holds you in its grip and can easily stop you getting better. I was anxious and forgetful.

The house was familiar but strange. I had visited it for a short while a few days earlier with two occupational therapists. They had wanted to know if I'd be able to get to the toilet, make a cup of tea, get out of my chair and wash myself. They watched me closely. They reckoned I could, just about. I didn't stop long that time, just long enough to realise that I needn't have worried about our only loo being upstairs. I had lain in bed in the hospital for several nights, really bothered that if I was eating downstairs and wanted to go to the loo, I wouldn't have the strength and speed to get all the way up the stairs in time. I'd wet myself. I was going to broach the idea with Emma of converting the cupboard under the stairs into a little downstairs loo. But now, with the occupational therapists, there was a revelation! We already had a downstairs loo! It's just that I had forgotten it was there. 'There's a downstairs loo?' I asked in wonder. 'Yes,' Emma said, in a quiet voice that I've imagined ever since as dreading what kind of impaired person was coming back for good a few days later.

Yes, what kind of person was I, then? Now that I've put some distance between this person drifting through no-man's-land time – the period between the coma and becoming as fit and as conscious as I'll ever be – it has grown in my mind to be something distinct and unknowable. I was a person who was bewildered but unable to say why I was bewildered; confused but unable to know what I was confused about; aware of how I felt from second to second but unable to find words to talk about it. I think of this time like this: I was confused. I was confused about being confused. People told me what had happened to me. I forgot what they told me. Then I forgot that I had forgotten.

I had words, but they were mostly medical: venti-lated, intubated, sedated. They were 'outside-in' words; how people had talked about what they had done to me. And I didn't even really know what they meant. I had hardly any words to talk about what I thought from the 'inside-out'.

One moment kept coming back to me from the ten days I was 'on the wards', after I came out of intensive care and before I was shipped off to the rehabilitation hospital. What with the huge pressure on beds in June 2020, I had been put into a geriatric ward. I was on one side in an alcove, so I couldn't see the other patients, but from what I now know of geriatric wards, the patients were in a very different state from mine. I could hear nurses talking to them with loud, slow voices. These were people, I fear, who were not far from death. As far as I know, they didn't think I was. The moment that kept coming back to me was when a nurse stood by my bed and said, 'What are you in here for anyway?'

I remember thinking, *I don't know. I have no idea why I'm in here. Aren't I in here because you think I should be in here? I'm not in here because I want a holiday. And if you don't know why I'm in here and I don't know why I'm in here, what are we going to do?*

There was no answer to this question. That was a lonely place to be.

The fact is, no one quietly explained to me that I had been unconscious for 40 days and that for a period after that (the period I was in right then, in fact) I'd be so confused I might be delirious. They told me that I might have hallucinations and delusions but no one told me exactly why. Or if they did, I didn't hear it and probably needed to be told many times. The lack of knowledge and understanding left me vulnerable, unable to make much progress.

I lay in bed puzzling over why I couldn't stand up. One day, two guys with Liverpudlian accents came to my bed and said that they were going to get me to walk. They grabbed me, propped me up and coaxed me to move a leg. I panicked, gasped with a ghastly rasp, shook and shuddered. I glanced down and saw two white spindly legs. *The legs my father had when he was dying*, I thought. The Liverpool guys gave up and put me back to bed.

I was shocked at my physical condition. I don't remember anyone explaining that 40 days on my back, doing nothing much else but breathe and digest the stuff they were pouring into me takes its toll: it wastes you. Whole chunks of your body give up, go to pot, go spongey. I was just doing what bodies do when that happens. It would have been good if someone had quietly explained to me that I wouldn't always be like that.

Things changed when I got to the rehabilitation hospital. Everything there was about progress. There was no time or reason to look back. Anyway, the people helping me to progress didn't seem to know about what had gone before. That had all happened in the other hospital. They had a wasted body in front of them and it was their job to get it going. A garage mechanic is not usually desperately interested in how you smashed your car. They want to know whether it can be repaired. Fair enough. I found this refreshing: the idea of looking forward and making progress, rather than fretting as I looked back.

But taking even small steps was challenge enough, given I couldn't yet walk. There was a funny side to this. I realised that the people teaching me how to stand up and walk had very different methods: one was a guy who had been in the Greek army. He would be very brisk and a bit hand-clappy: 'One, two, three, let's go!' The others would be a bit like nursery school teachers: 'Would you like to see if you can lift your legs out of the bed, Michael?' I called them hard cop, soft cop. Actually, at the time it was exciting. Every day, I moved forward: from bed to Zimmer, from Zimmer to wheelchair, from wheelchair to stick. I pedalled away on an exercise bike. I walked between parallel bars. I picked up a balloon and threw it and it felt like I was throwing a rock. I saw myself as a hero (sorry about that!) when I reached a new level: like the day I got from my bed to the loo without a stick. Wahay! (I sang M People's hit 'Search for the Hero Inside Yourself' to myself to get to the loo. Why not?)

Why am I going on about this? Because I'm amazed by it. What an incredible thing the body is. If you do the right things at the right time for the right length of time, you can get better. Of course, of course, of course, I wasn't doing this on my own. I had the full wisdom, training and experience of the people at the rehabilitation hospital – physiotherapists, occupational therapists, nurses and doctors teaching me. That's what they do. They cared for me and they taught me. And they gave me homework: exercises, practice routines. And they told me that I would get better. I remember asking Ashima, an occupational therapist, what training she had done. An MSc, she said. That's a masters in science, and here she was, playing throw-the-balloon with me. What she was doing was funnelling all that knowledge into the activity that was the right one for me in my condition in my state of progress. She was turning her knowledge of muscle blocks, balance, rates of progress and the all-important matter of motivation into one simple silly activity for me. To have that kind of support and help is precious. I don't think I would have got from where I was to where I am now, as fast as I did, without this.

The core thing I take from this therapy is this: the medics did things *to me* and gave me drugs to help me get better. Physiotherapists and occupational therapists gave me methods to use myself, in the process of getting better. All the time that I was doing what they asked me to do, they were also giving me tools to take *with me*, long past the time they would be there to tell me what to do. It's easy to think of physical therapy as exercises given by others to do to your body – outside-in, if you like. In fact, what the therapists were teaching me was how to put myself into the right frame of mind so that I could do all sorts of different kinds of exercise depending on the time or day or whatever else was going on in my life – inside-out, then, and I can't emphasise enough how important this was. I saw it going on in the rehab hospital around me. Some people immediately reverted back to being at school, and turned the therapists into schoolteachers. They worked out ways to be 'naughty' or bunk off, without realising that they were really bunking off from themselves. The best way to get the most out of any form of physiotherapy is to figure out how you're going to carry on when the physiotherapist is not there. In fact, the best physios are the ones who know that their job is not to get you fit, but to show you how you can get yourself fit. When I realised this, it was a lightbulb moment.

On one occasion, I said to one of the physios in the rehab hospital (also an Emma) that I didn't think I would ever be strong enough to stand in front of 500 or a 1,000 children telling them stories, making them laugh, as I had done again and again for the previous 40 years. 'Oh, don't be so sure about that,' they said, 'you will.' I thought that was nice of them, cheering me on, encouraging me like that. Inside, I was pretty sure that I wouldn't. And yet some 15 months later, I stood on a theatre stage for an hour in front of 500 children, telling them my poems and stories, hearing the laughter coming back at me. All the time I was doing it, in the back of my mind, I was thinking of the occupational therapists. Even as I was doing my poems, inside my mind I was saying to the therapists, 'You were right. I was wrong!'

After the show I was signing books and someone was standing in front of me, with a mask on, saying, 'It's me.' I looked. It was Emma. I reminded her what she had said to me in the gym and that I had been thinking of that moment even as she and her children had been in the audience a few minutes earlier. I held out my hands and said, 'It worked. I did it!'

I realise that in telling you this, I've circled to and fro between the intensive care ward, the geriatric ward, the rehabilitation hospital and coming home. That's what it's like. That's what I do a lot of the time in daily life as I go about doing my things. It's as if my mind is a mixture in a bottle that's been shaken up. Maybe it's a vinaigrette: oil, vinegar, herbs, spices, garlic. You shake it up and it all merges. Leave it for a while and it settles and separates into all its different ingredients. Yes, that's what I've been doing. That's part of getting better too: waiting for everything to separate, settle and become clear about what's there. Give it time, Michael, give it time.

I've got some other ingredients to add to this recipe for recovery.

Once I came home, a heavy realisation hit me: I had nearly died. There was a moment just before I was sedated when a doctor stood over me and asked if I would sign a piece of paper that would let them put me to sleep. 'Will I wake up?' I said. 'There's a fifty-fifty chance,' he said. 'If I don't sign?' I asked.

'Zero,' he said. I wrote about this in *Many Different Kinds of Love*, leaving out what I was actually thinking. I'll tell you what I was thinking: *Fifty-fifty? That's not too bad. Definitely better than zero.* Maybe I was already high on opiates or just high on lack of oxygen, but that's what I thought.

Now, I hear what I thought inside my head or read it on the page and I have a feeling of dread. I realise that I was going into a situation where the best minds available at that moment didn't know if I'd come out alive. I've found out since that that doctor was more or less right. In my ward, 42 per cent of us died. We were the first round of Covid patients. Our lungs and brains were full of blood clots and haemorrhages, our immune reaction was playing havoc with our lungs and organs. The consultant later told me about the three blood clots sitting in the 'saddle' of my pulmonary arteries. The pulmonary artery leaves the heart, and once it gets above it, it divides in two to head off to the two sides of our lungs. The point where they branch is the 'saddle'. I often think of those little lumps of clotted blood sitting in there. If the clots moved too much, they could have got blocked in one of the nooks and crannies of the heart and stopped it altogether. Or, they could have got to my brain and knocked out chunks of it. But they didn't. Amazing. Sometimes, it's important to realise that there's a degree of randomness in all this, and that, especially when it comes to our bodies, not everything is within our conscious control.

It often seems incredible to me that our bodies seem to make life and death decisions for us without us ever knowing about it. Under sedation, in the coma, my body could have just given up. My consultant, Professor Hugh Montgomery, told me later that with intensive care patients, he can be having a chat with them one moment, then he might pop out for a cup of tea, and when he comes back, they're gone. It's touch and go for days, weeks, months. In my case, it was nearly six weeks. I was part of a film exploring the effect the coronavirus had on hospitals, their patients and their staff – *2020: The Story of Us*. In the film, Professor Montgomery said something that he didn't tell me at the time: 'We didn't know if Michael was going to be brain-dead or not.' As I heard him say that on film, I nearly jumped out of my chair. He was saying that my blank, dilated left eye staring at him seemed to indicate that a chunk of my brain had died? *Really? Wow. I never knew.*

In the film, he also comes to my bed and says, 'Michael, you've got children.' I look at him and say with a slight smile, 'Apparently.' I have no memory of this at all. It's almost as if I really was brain-dead! Did I think I was being funny? Was I expressing in some sideways way that I didn't know where my children were, nor why I wasn't with them? Perhaps.

I try to work out what all this stuff means. I feel that I have to in order to get better. Maybe others could just accept it, rather like I accept that people who service our car fiddle around in there with all their years of experience and hand it back to us in good nick. When it comes to me and my body, though, I want to know more. On the one hand, I can look at it on film, recall what people said, and write about it as if it's happened to someone else. But feeling it on the inside is harder. I can find it sad, and I can even find it funny. I wrote about me visiting the Land of the Dead, like Odysseus in *The Odyssey*. He cheats the gods, gets in, and gets out again. *That was me*, I thought. Then someone said to me, 'You were the Resurrection of the Year.' Why not? Nice one. I tell other people, 'I was the Resurrection of the Year.' They laugh. I feel better. I've made the unthinkable bearable. I don't feel dread, thinking about it, now I've learned more about it all.

In the rehabilitation hospital, I had learned about the power of physical activity to help my recovery. At home, I tried to continue this: I walked and walked and walked. There are all sorts of cures for mind or body but one of the best is walking. The slow rhythm, the sense of progress across the landscape or city-scape, the space you give yourself to think all help you feel good (in many ways, it reminds me of when I discovered running on Hackney Marshes all those years ago, helping me after my hypothyroid diagnosis). You can feel yourself getting stronger too. At first, I did round and round the garden. I even played round and round the garden like a teddy bear with my granddaughter when she came over. Then I walked the block around the streets where I live. I called these 'laps'. I went from one to two, two to three, three to four laps. We live in a hilly part of town so you know whenever you walk down, you'll have to walk up to get home. I started doing this: across the park, down the hill, up the hill. When I did my visit to the 'brain hospital', the nurse asked me how much exercise I do. I proudly said three 30-minute walks a week. She said, 'It should be five.' Now, I build those five walks into my work schedule, walking to work, walking back if I can. Remember the hills!

Emma, meanwhile, bridged the gap between hospital and home, doing the blood-thinner jabs into the fat roll round my middle, tolerating me peeing in a bottle for the first few nights, cutting my toenails – hell, they were a long way away – and making sure the district nurse came over to dress the hole in my neck where they stuck the tracheostomy in. She ferried me to and from the hospital for the audiologists and ophthalmologists to poke and probe in my ear and eye. Lucky me. Having someone to focus on these practical aspects meant the burden was taken off my shoulders.

She said, 'We sort the things out one by one.' How simple and true was that! When we're all shook up, as I was, we need reassurance. I was very lucky to get it. In my mind, there were hundreds of bits of me that had gone wrong: ear, eye, toes, neck, dizziness, lips, skin, leg pain, joint pain, chest pain . . . on and on and on. 'We sort the things out one by one.' I love that, and I try to apply it now when I'm overwhelmed.

So, does it matter I nearly died? In the long run of things, no. If I had died, it wouldn't matter at all to me. Now that I've lived, it's very nice to be here. (Or is it that's it's nice to be back?) So come on, lad (as my father used to say to me), there's no need to keep going over it. I often say, 'Come on, lad!' to myself. It's both a comfort and a reminder not to worry myself too much, to sort things out one by one, and take those small steps forward.

Emma's care was one of many forms that I was lucky enough to experience. There were others. One day, Emma said, 'The nurses in intensive care kept a diary.' She pointed at it on the kitchen table. A small black notebook, with little metal rings holding it together. It has a label on it, marked 'Patient Diary' (or 'Very patient diary', as I call it). There are about 50 or so pages filled with nurses' handwriting, dates and names. They're letters to me for most of the days I was unconscious. We put a good few of them in my book, *Many Different Kinds of Love*, but I'll let you into a secret: I couldn't bear to read them. Instead, I glanced at them, and skim-read them in that way you do when you don't want to take in the full meaning. I didn't want to face up to the truth that they were people saving my life, looking at me inert in a bed, day after day, night after night. I even resisted editing them for the book, to save me having to pore over their meaning: I left it to the editor.

But I got round to it in the end. As I read the diary, I discovered that a whole group of nurses and doctors stood round my bed on 7 May and sang me 'Happy Birthday'. Really? Did they? I read how I got 'agitated' or how they shaved my beard off so that the tracheostomy wound didn't get septic. I have read how they wished me well, over and over again.

This is care. I've said that it reminds me of what parents do, when our children are ill. We give our children what we think will make them better but then we go the extra mile – we sing to them, we stroke their foreheads, we sit by their beds. We call it love. The nurses did all this. They did it for me. Saw me out the door and then did it for other patients again and again. They're doing it right now. I am in awe and gratitude. It makes me feel good to think about it and to express that gratitude. Whether it's their training or the people they are, or both, it's what has helped me live. That's something to treasure.

Other people sense this when they've read the letters in my book. In fact, one or two friends have said that the letters are the best part of it. I'll take that. Ever since the 1960s, I've been a fan of the voices of working people in documentaries, storytelling or singing. And here I was in the book, being a channel for putting that sort of thing into the public's hands to read. There was something cathartic in sharing these words, as if they were part of a bigger recovery – not just mine, but that of the whole country as it tried to come back from a trauma. Words can be powerful healers too.

One of the nurses sent me the journal he kept while he worked in the hospital, including while I was in there. He changed all the names. He called me 'Mr Jacobs'. One entry says, 'Today I say a few hail marys over Mr Jacobs, even though he's Jewish.' A few days later, he describes himself walking into the ward one morning. He writes, 'Mr Jacobs is still alive.' I keep reading this. There's Mr Jacobs not knowing that a nurse cares enough about him to share his culture's bit of well-wishing with me. And then he shows me just how on the edge of life I was. He had gone home at the end of his shift and didn't know if Mr Jacobs would last the night. He comes in in the morning, and I'm hanging on in there. As I read that, I thought, *Well done, Mr Jacobs!* And then I remember that's me.

I'm Mr Jacobs. And it was thanks to nurses like him that Mr Jacobs made it. That feels great.

Do you see a pattern here? As I learn more, and think more, about my illness, I keep chalking up things to feel good about. That's a big part of getting better. It's like a form of physio: doing and thinking things that make you feel better, because sure enough there are loads of things that make you feel bad! It's my 'One Good Thing Principle'. It goes like this: try to do one thing every day that makes you proud. It can be very small, like shopping for what you want to eat, paying a bill, learning a song, going for a walk, cooking something nice, helping someone, organising something, taking part in something that gets things done or makes a point – anything. Then, as you go to sleep, fix your mind on it. Just focus on that one good thing, so that the bad things, the ones that make you feel scared or fed up, don't crowd your mind. Allow yourself to be proud of it. Allow yourself to say to yourself, 'I did that.' You don't have to tell anyone else about it either. It's your thought for yourself. It's for you. I really believe in this.

I also believe in keeping yourself busy in other ways, and for me, this was work. I'm lucky enough to enjoy what I do, and am my own boss, whereas I'm very aware that others might not be as fortunate. Even so, I hope you can find ways to make some of this next part work for you. Maybe you can take what

I call 'work' and apply it to whatever you like doing: cooking, gardening, knitting, swimming, working on your family tree – anything active, productive, enjoyable. Especially helpful, I think, are things where you can see progress, where things develop, get made, or grow, because you can grow alongside them.

Writing, which is my job and for many is a hobby, is a great example of this. When I was in bed in the hospital, I couldn't write. To begin with it was because I couldn't hold a tablet or laptop and type, nor could I hold a pen and notebook for longer than a minute or so. Instead, I made up stories in my head. I remembered that I had once had the idea of a cat called Rigatoni. Rigatoni would be a cat that loved pasta: Rigatoni the Pasta Cat. Yes, that's it, and I thought about how two people look after Rigatoni, give him all the pasta he likes. (I love the sound of the pasta names and as I lay in bed with my memory shot to bits, I enjoyed trying to remember them: spaghetti, macaroni, fusilli, penne . . . *and what's that one that's like butterflies? I'll ask Emma next time we're on the phone* . . . and so it went on.) I imagined how maybe the two people have to go away and a boy comes every day to feed Rigatoni . . . but the people who look after him forget to tell him that Rigatoni loves pasta! Problem. Dilemma. It's what writers call 'jeopardy' or 'peril': the moment where your hero lacks something, or is in trouble, or in a fix. I had it.

Rigatoni has no pasta. What does he do? This is how I thought as I lay in bed.

In the end, I made up a whole story. When I came home, Emma warned me not to work. She had bought me a lovely sunbed and told me that I had to lie in it. I did. But I also wanted to see if I really could write another story. Or was my mind shot to bits? I sat down and wrote out *Rigatoni the Pasta Cat* and sent it off to the publishers of my other little animal stories. Yes! The editor liked it! I was back on track.

You can see what I did there: I did some thinking, I went into a kind of daydream, I thought about what I might do or could do. I planned. Then I got the materials necessary to put the plan into practice. I worked away at it to get it right. I showed someone else to see if they liked it. And they did. That little pattern or cycle can be copied for all the things we do: cooking, making something, even potentially very boring things like shopping. We can think of them as growth, progress – achievements even.

Later, I found that people wanted to meet me on Zoom. In a way, I was very lucky. The world had slowed down for me. Instead of having to rush off to studios, school, publishers and college, I could do it all from home. I rode on a wave of 'getting things done'. I think that this was crucial for me to feel that I was making progress. I also think that if I had been asked to slot back into my old way of working, dashing about all over the country, I would have had to say no, and I would have missed out on what matters for me, what makes me tick. Instead, work was a great healer.

And I started to do new things: new ways of writing, new ways of using the technology, new bits of research. Novelty can be a great healer too. You get the joy and reward of finding out something new. One example: in 2021, my father's cousin Michael died. He was 97, the only Holocaust survivor in Europe on the Rosen side of the family. At least six of my father's uncles and aunts were killed in Auschwitz. Michael survived because his mother and father put him on a train from western Poland to eastern Poland. He never saw them again. The Russians, who were occupying eastern Poland, put him into a labour camp – horrible, but not as terrible as an extermination camp. While he was in eastern Poland and in the Russian labour camp, his parents wrote to him. He joined the Polish Free Army, marched and fought with them over thousands of miles and in the end got to England, where he lived for the next 75 years or so.

Michael's sons and I talked about the letters his parents sent to him. They are in Polish, they said. Did they know what the letters say? I asked. They didn't. I understand that. It's not easy and maybe not appropriate to dive in and ask to see such things, let alone get a stranger to come along and translate them.

Nevertheless, I asked them if they thought it would be OK to get them translated. I know people who would be able to do that. Yes, now would be a good time, they thought. So one of the sons came over with a little stained canvas bag. Inside were more than 20 worn, faded cards, with Polish and Russian stamps on them, addresses in eastern Poland and the Russian labour camp. I found someone to translate them and a few weeks later, they came back. The letters are full of pleas from Michael's mother and father for him to write, questions about how he's doing. It's awful to think that he was 16 and 17 when they were written. Sad and overwhelming though they are, it was nevertheless a good thing to get them translated for Michael's sons and for the rest of the family to see. In 1941, the letters stop. I went to my computer and searched for the name of the town where Michael's parents were living. In 1941, the Nazis created a ghetto for all the Jews of the town. By the end of 1941, the ghetto was 'liquidated'.

In a way, this is all work too, even if it's not work in the usual sense. This was work that was fulfilling, rewarding and made links between people in our family. There was also an element of discovery about it, that we were uncovering stuff that was new and relevant to our lives. It mattered to a whole group of us. And we could match the personal stories of the

family with the wider (and awful) story of what happened to thousands of others in the same situation. I
feel guilty saying that this was 'satisfying', but it was a
way of using what I've got (education, contacts, per-
sistence) to achieve something that gave others a
feeling of resolution. It felt good to do this.

In spite of these activities, which help to keep me
feeling good, I can't escape my body entirely. These
days, I have my 'Pinball Pain'. Whether it's from
Covid or because I'm in my seventies or both, I have
what's become a joke of mine: pains (or creaks,
twinges, cramps, sorenesses) seem to ping about my
body like a pinball in a pinball game. The moment
one twinge fades in my ankle, another pops up in my
neck. One pain dies, another pops up. Some of these
can be quite acute. Some of them can last for weeks
on end and then disappear. On any given day, I do
hundreds of little things to keep them at bay. There's
a scene in the old version of *The Jungle Book* that I had
as a child, where a pack of wild dogs do some attacking.
When one dog gets pushed away, another one dives in
somewhere else. That's how I see my pinball pains.

To tell the truth, when I disperse one of these
twinges, I become ludicrously proud. Let's say it's a
pain at the base of my spine. I've done classes and
read books on back pain. I know some tricks to do

with breathing, bending my knees, stretching, lying on the floor on my back and gently pulling my knees up to my chest and so on. If a combination of these works, I spend the next few hours telling myself I did good!

If a qualified practitioner tells me of something that can help me with a pain or twinge, I ask them why and how it will help. If I'm convinced, I do it. Covid attacked my toes and I lost my big toenails. I remember looking down at my feet in the geriatric ward and wondering why there were red scabs where my big toenails had been. We now know that Covid attacks some of the cells in the veins, arteries and the tiny blood vessels called capillaries. These cells produce stuff that prevents our blood from clotting. If they are killed off by Covid, our blood clots in our blood vessels. The clots in the capillaries will kill off the capillaries. Some people have lost their toes. In my case it was just the big toenails and, as it happens, the feeling in my toes too. It also caused haemorrhages in my brain, but as far as I know that didn't kill my brain off.

So, over the next year, my big toenails grew back. The problem is that one of them decided to grow into my toe. I made several trips to a podiatrist and they did heroïc things, like digging out chunks of skin and nail. All good, but it was still sore. Then the podiatrist said, 'You're old. The skin on your feet hardens. Skin is hardening on your toes at the point

where the nail curves into the toe. You've got to mois-
ten your toes in olive oil.' He said that there's a
substance in olive oil that will soften your skin and
you won't keep having these pains and soreness. And
it can be any old olive oil. You don't have to do extra-
virgin cold-pressed, he said! I thought of people in
the Bible and in ancient Greek literature having their
feet 'anointed' with oil. They knew something.

So that's what I started to do. It's been miraculous.

I love this sort of thing: remedies recommended
by someone who knows how to keep the pinball pain
at bay. If we were sitting in a room and you trusted
me and I trusted you, I would also tell you about piles.
I came out of hospital with piles. A lot of the books
and websites will tell you that you can't get rid of piles
or that you have to use this or that medicine, or that
if it gets terrible, you have to have an op. All I'll say is
that I have done things that have got rid of my piles
and it makes me proud to say that I've done that. I
got better and feel better. Result!

But I also have to resign myself to things that
won't get better. In all this stuff, we can make positive
strides, but we have to dose ourselves with lashings of
realism. If we have something that won't get better,
we have to try to accept it. As I became aware of
where I was after the intensive care ward, I realised
that I couldn't see very well with my left eye or hear
very well with my left ear. They were, in their own

ways, both fogged. I try not to say that I can't hear with my left eye or that I can't see with my left ear, because it seems defeatist and not as funny as I hope. But, actually, that's what it feels like! Foggy and muddled. I sometimes walk into walls. When someone talks on my left side, I sometimes hear it on my right. I look the wrong way to see who's talking. It looks like a comedy routine.

I hoped that this would get better. I've had loads of 'procedures' on my eye: laser, cataract, 'XEN', drops . . . but it's still foggy. I have to say to myself, 'That's it, it's not going to get better, lad.' (There's my dad again!) It's not easy. There are times that I feel sorry for myself. I almost feel as if I've been punished for something. That's the irrational paranoid stuff kicking in again. If I work on the rational stuff and say, my eye and ear got knocked out by micro clots in my brain, I've got an explanation to think about. In a way, I'm a pioneer in the history of Covid. Things happened to me early on in the pandemic that have come to be seen as part of consequences going on worldwide, and I can use that to make me feel more positive.

And I have one good eye and one good ear. I've worked with children who have neither. It's humbling to see them cope. When I start to be a bit self-pitying – or 'drivelly', as I call it – I remind myself of their strength and humour.

Chapter 10

Words

Occasionally, I am asked by newspapers and the like to offer up a message on 'coping'. How do you cope, they ask me? Or what's your philosophy of life, or some such? Sometimes they fire binaries at me: optimist or pessimist? These questions have, at the very least, the advantage of making me think: what actually is it all for? What kind of person am I? In this book, you'll have seen I'm a 'doer', and that the act of making small steps can help keep bad things at bay. But I also have another theory, and it's one I shared with the *Observer* in December 2021:

'Play is what makes life bearable.'

In the piece, I elaborate on this. Staying silly has always been important to me, it comes from my strong sense of the absurd. The way I see it, there really isn't much reason why we're on Earth. When we're focussed entirely on daily troubles and chores, we don't notice it's all ultimately pointless. So why not try to look for fun, while it lasts?

It's easy to be drawn into the doom of human existence, especially when you have suffered with illness or grief. I have to remind myself that there's no point in spending a life being totally miserable. At first, when bad things happen, it's hard not to think of the world as having been spoiled. Instead, I now try to focus on how I'm still evolving. Deciphering the world is a whole new challenge, it needn't be melancholic. It's an adventure, a strange new game.

Play, for me, is what makes life bearable, when we're walking, shopping, working, letting our minds run free and wild. For me, much of the time, that means playing with words. I discovered when my son died that I'm less bothered by things if I write about them. Some writing is straightforwardly light-hearted and jolly. But penning a poem about sadness or a sense of loss can leave you feeling better as well. It helps, laying things down on paper. I call it 'unfolding'.

Everyone can do this, it doesn't take expertise. Think of it as doodling, but with words. There's a tyranny to education: learning to write frees you, but we're restricted by being taught that formal sentences are all that's worthwhile. Instead, scribble down fragments – think up half-lines mixed with song lyrics, lines from films, things people say. Don't over-think it – it's like talking with your pen. This process is a liberation for the mind.

That was the advice I gave in that interview, and I stand by it. What also keeps me going is being curious and staying curious. I keep wanting to know what's going on, how things work, why people say the stuff they say, why they do what they do. I keep wanting to know about the past and what's going on now, what's going on far away or near. Again, writing can be a brilliant way of making sense of all this.

I want to show you what I mean by this in more detail. There are a lot of guides to writing and most of them are about helping people to write better. That's great. But what I'm talking about is some-thing slightly different: writing to feel better, writing to get better.

It may be that doing this does help you to write better too, but that's a perk, a side benefit, if you like.

Let's start with 'playing with words' to get better. We use words because they mean something. I say 'light bulb' and I mean the light bulb I'm going to put into my light socket. I may also say, 'I've had a light-bulb moment', and that's what we call a 'metaphor' as part of 'figurative' language. Generally, there's a shared meaning that we understand. But let's ask the question, where is the meaning of words? Who owns the meaning of words? It's not in dictionaries, but in our minds, between us. The meaning of 'light bulb', and all words, are agreements we have with the people around us. We agree (without having to say anything) that this thing I call a light bulb is also what you call a light bulb. But the meaning also depends on other things: the context, the speaker, the genre of writing, and the history of a word – the way meaning evolves over time.

This applies to words generally, but also us specifically, and how you yourself have heard and used the word in your lifetime. This has been described as words being able to 'denote' – they mean something specific, have some kind of core meaning – while for each of us words they also have 'connotations' – that is, connections with our own personal lives in hundreds of different ways. (The first thing that springs into my mind with 'light bulb' is the trade name of an old brand of them – 'Mazda', who was also the Persian god of light.)

What all this means is that words are ours. They belong to us. We don't have to ask the permission from a dictionary to use them. Once we find the freedom to play with words, we can often feel good as we speak and write. This may come simply from the fact that we are playing with words, and play feels great – liberating and enjoyable. These moments can be like islands of happiness in a sea of gloom!

The other crucial context for the meaning of a word is the words around it: what comes before it or after it; the wider phrase or sentence it's in; what we might expect to come next. A word in one sentence can mean something very different when it's in another. The word 'leg' can mean your lower limb, or it can mean one of two consecutive matches between the same teams in a football tournament. How do we know the difference? From the contexts. Quite a lot of the time, it's down to us to create these contexts. If we're feeling bad, quite often we have a sense of being out of control. Controlling what we write and how we write can give us back some control as we use words to recollect our experiences. This gives us agency, which we might sometimes feel we've lost.

When we write, we play with meaning but – and here's the thing – words have their own shape and sound, and these can be fun to play with too. They exist in the material world (as Madonna told us), whether that's on a page, a screen, on a poster, a road sign, on the side of a van, on a tombstone – or in the sound waves we produce with air and the vocal folds in our throats. Gestures and sign languages exist as physical movements using nerves, muscles and bones. We can play with the physical existence of words, their sounds, just as much as their meaning.

I could sit in a room with other people and we could

experiment with all the different ways we can say 'mel-ancholy'. We could break it up into different parts: melon, collie. Mel an' Collie. We could play my 'bacon slicer game', taking one letter off the front at a time:

> Melancholy,
> elancholy,
> lancholy,
> ancholy,
> ncholy,
> choly,
> holy,
> oly,
> ly,
> y.

This is me using a word purely in its physical way. And yet, as I do it, new meanings pop into view . . . There's a 'choly' in there, which I could pronounce as 'collie'; a 'holy' in there; 'ly', which I could pronounce as 'lie'; and 'y' as 'why?' Now I could practise that, chanting it with a rhythm . . . getting faster and faster.

Through playing with the sounds of 'melancholy', I've come up with new meanings inside the word. These meanings, and the process of getting to them, are not melancholy at all.

There are hundreds of ways to play with words. Here are a few of my favourites.

Advertisements and notices are full of games with fonts.

> *Private!*
> *NO SWIMMING ALLOWED!*

means something different from

> *Private?*
> *No!*
> *Swimming allowed.*

Another game I love to play involves words that sound the same (that is, in your accent) but mean different things. The way I say 'sore' sounds the same as the way I say 'saw'. (For people from, say, the USA or Scotland, they don't sound the same.) I can also say that soar sounds the same as sore. We can make lists of words like this, or make up puns, jokes and song lines for them. The first joke that I remember someone telling me was 'What are the strongest shellfish? Mussels.' Almost all jokes begin here, with a bit of wordplay.

It's something that children often do for fun, sometimes at school.

Someone put up a note on Twitter recently saying that their daughter needed to recite a poem at school about a giraffe or a narwhal. Lots of people took up the challenge of writing one. I couldn't resist:

> Would yer raffle a giraffe?
> A giraffe'll raffle a giraffe
> if a giraffe haff a raffle
> an' the raffle's for a giraffe.

When I say this one, I cheat a bit by saying 'would-yer' as 'wouldj-yer', and as you can see I've made 'have' into 'haff', as some English speakers do. This brings the sounds of the tongue-twister nearer together and therefore easier to muddle! Maybe you could make one that's harder to say by using words like 'rattle', 'faff', 'graph', 'jaffa', 'half', 'rafter', and so on.

As adults, though, we can often lose sight of games like this, which might have stimulated and entertained us when we were younger.

So why spend time on them? For a similar reason, I guess, to why we doodle, be it drawing, painting, using clay, working out dance moves, flower-arranging or whatever. More specifically, it's for the same reason we play with words in crosswords, play Scrabble or even games like charades, Pictionary, Boggle, Wordle, or that old card game Lexicon. Words are powerful things. We use them for most of the things we do; we use them for a good deal of our thinking. We define ourselves and others with words. We try to influence each other with words. We suggest, grieve, love, laugh with words. They last in our heads for decades. New ones crop up all the time.

In other words, words are important. (That last sentence was nearly a joke.)

Some people get a bit irritated by this kind of play. They want words to do bigger, deeper emotional things. A lot of what I've said in this book has been with words trying to do just that. Along the way, I've tried to say, 'You have a go at this too. Copy what I'm doing here – it'll help you feel better and get better.' And I do think that, by reclaiming the fun of words, we can learn to express ourselves more effectively on the 'bigger', more serious questions too.

Finding your voice can be hard. So how might we do it?

One way is to start with what other people say.

I noticed when I was in hospital, doctors and nurses kept coming to my bedside and saying 'You were poorly' or 'You were very poorly'. As you can see, it's not exactly a technical medical word. I was quite tickled by it. What did they mean? Were they saying that I was a *bit* ill, or was it a way to hide that they were saying I had been *very, very* ill? At that stage, as they were saying it, they meant that I was nearly a goner, I nearly died. At the time, though, I just thought they meant that I was pretty ill, like the way you feel when you've got a fever or something. Anyway, I jotted down 'very poorly'. Just that.

Now, when I say that you can 'unfold' this kind of writing, it means that you don't have to put 'very poorly' into a sentence. It's just there on the page. Then you think what you might write underneath it. That's the important bit. You write it somewhere else, perhaps underneath. So next, I wrote:

> It's something they say about me.

Notice that I'm writing it as if it's happening now – in the present. Sometimes this is a good way for something to feel immediate.

I then unfolded the next bit, to explain to me and to anyone reading it:

> Every so often a doctor or nurse
> stands by my bed and says,
> 'You were very poorly.'

Notice again how I unfold the phrases, one under the other. It helps me to think logically and to write in a kind of spoken voice: 'talking with my pen' as I call it. 'Write it like I say it,' I say to myself.

On I go:

> I'm starting to expect it.

Notice that this is the first time I say anything about how I feel. This way of writing doesn't have to try very hard to express feeling. As a way of writing, I hope that the feeling comes out from the detail and from the context – which may be the poems or pictures near to it (more on that in a moment).

On I go with my observations of the doctors and nurses:

> They often seem pleased – surprised almost –
> that I'm less poorly.

This is about thinking of oddities or ironies or contrasts. Every situation has little moments of tension, cross-currents of feeling or image that might clash with another. I've unfolded that. Hiding behind that word 'surprised' is perhaps their expectation that I might have died. But notice: I don't say that yet! Also, notice how I interrupt myself. I say, '– surprised almost –'. This gives me a way of adding thoughts together or arguing with myself.

> I get the feeling that some people
> who were very poorly, died.

Here I'm widening it out from just me. I'm thinking about those other people in my ward. It brings them into the 'picture' of the poem.

Last line:

> I didn't die.

This is a bit of absurdism, or wry or 'sardonic' humour. I've said elsewhere in the book that it's how some people (and me) cope. If in this poem I had expressed amazement or horror that I had nearly died, it would have (I think) sounded too self-pitying. I do sometimes pity myself, but it's quite an unattractive thing to display to others or even to myself. Better to cheer myself up with a bit of this dry, ironic way of writing, I tell myself. Of course I didn't die, I'm writing this stuff down on the page, aren't I?!

Here's the finished poem:

> Very poorly.
> It's something they say about me.
> Every so often a doctor or nurse
> stands by my bed and says,
> 'You were very poorly.'
> I'm starting to expect it.
> They often seem pleased – surprised almost –
> that I'm less poorly.
> I get the feeling that some people
> who were very poorly, died.
> I didn't die.

So that's it. That's the little poem. You see that it started from something that people said to me. I told it how and where it was told to me. I widened it out to others in my situation and then saw something absurd about why I was going on about it. I did that by unfolding it, line by line, and doing that helped me to process that small part of my experience, all by reflecting on that word 'poorly', which had been used by others about me, and which I now claimed for myself in the poem: agency again.

That's it. End of poem. No need to fill the page. Start a new page with a new thought. The next page begins quite differently:

I'm wearing mittens . . .

Another in-the-moment bit of unfolding . . .

The 'very poorly' poem is sitting in a book in amongst a lot of other things: drawings by the wonderful Chris Riddell, letters from the nurses who looked after me in intensive care, the letter from the doctor who came and took my oxygen level and realised that I was nearly gone, emails from Emma to the family about me in hospital, and more of these 'unfolded' thoughts, memories and observations. So on the one hand the 'poorly' poem stands alone, but also, it enjoys the company of these other kinds of writing. They cast shadows over this poem, and this poem casts shadows over the others. It's as if they are each parts of a stained-glass window and we look at the mix of lights on the floor below the window as the sun shines through: different colours blurring into each other, but they each originate with a separate bit of glass. It's one way to write, if you want to. I like doing that. It helps me gather up what has happened to me.

It's a scrapbook. I'm very lucky to have had it published, but anyone can make a scrapbook: a mix of drawings, things that people say, letters, texts, leaflets, train tickets, photos and so on. It's a way of documenting who we are, where we are, how we are at a particular time.

Now, you might ask, how does that make you feel better or get better?

Well, go back to my state of mind when I wrote it. I was feeling very weak and very muddled. Emma had explained to me several times that I had been in a coma for 40 days but I had no memory of this. Instead, I had blurred memories of being in several different wards, being wheeled down corridors, having brief chats with nurses and doctors. I couldn't match these blurred memories with the timeline that Emma was giving me. Secretly, I was becoming distressed about it. I didn't want to burden Emma with what I thought was a bit silly compared to the immensity of nearly dying, but the muddle was bothering me. At times, it felt nightmarish. So I wrote fragments like this 'Very poorly' piece. The images of nurses and doctors using the phrase loomed up in my mind. I grabbed the images and fixed them on the page. This made me feel better. I had somehow got hold of them, proved to myself that they happened, and I played with that phrase 'very poorly' as it came back to me over and over again. Before writing it down, I couldn't control that muddled, nightmarish feeling. When I wrote it down, I did get control over it. That's one way that writing makes me feel better, and get better.

Another way of writing is to look at things around us closely. The more closely we look, the more things start to come up that remind us of other things, creating patterns. If the thing we're looking at changes, that may remind us of changes in our own lives. If things seem to be very permanent, that may contrast with the fact that everything else seems to be changing.

These elements – looking closely, noticing patterns, being reminded of other things, noticing change, noticing contrasts – are very fruitful ways of writing. They help us concentrate and help us see 'things in the world; the world in things'.

Let me give you an example. I wrote:

> I walk the beach
> testing each step
> for safe enough sand:
> fear of toppling.
> I make it to the cliff,

> look up at its massiveness.
> A child
> leaps from one rock to the next,
> hulks in the sand
> ignoring her whoops of delight.
> The sea gets on with
> doing what it's always done.
> A week later
> the News tells of a cliff fall.
> It was at that beach.

The surface meaning is simple: I'm at the beach. I go for a walk. I notice some stuff around me: a cliff, a child, the sea. Then a week later, there was a cliff fall. The end. Now ask, why do that? Why put one thing next to another like that? (This is called 'juxtaposition'.) Every juxtaposition, in writing or in life, produces a meaning other than the two things being put next to each other. If I write:

> *Table*
> *Orange*

there'll be a new meaning to do with where and when these two things are. Many of us will guess that the orange is on the table. But I didn't say that.

Now, go back to me on the beach and pick up the 'characteristics' of each of us there: I'm 'testing each step', I'm afraid of 'toppling', I 'make it' to the cliff. So I'm weak and not walking very well, and fearful. There's a child who of course is young and active, leaping and whooping.

Meanwhile the cliff is 'massive' and the sea is being permanent, 'doing what it's always done'.

So we have contrasts here: me, child, cliff and sea.

Then a week later the news comes in which mucks all this up, disrupts it. The cliff has fallen down. So: not so permanent, eh? This is a small irony. I had thought that I was the one who was toppling but it turns out that one of the permanent things in that scene was the thing that toppled. Maybe what lasts in my mind better than the cliff, the sea or me, is the child leaping and whooping.

So this is another kind of writing, through close looking and 'juxtaposition'. Notice also that I don't say any of that stuff about 'contrasts' or 'irony' in the poem itself. I try to make the poem just 'be' while the reader can (if they want to) do the work to see or feel the juxtaposition. This is the 'less is more' principle. The way someone will be affected might be more, if the writer (me) says less. You'll see that I hardly used any emotion or feeling words like 'sad' or 'happy' or 'amazed'. There's 'fear' of toppling and that's about it.

I offer this as a way of writing about difficult and troubling things. I was, in truth, bewildered, sad and anxious about what had become of me when I wrote this in August 2020. I thought that I was an old crock, that my life was pretty well over, that I was doomed to have a strange, forgetful, muddled mind, an eye that couldn't see, an ear that couldn't hear. My teenage son was on the beach wanting to play footy with me and I couldn't kick a ball. I was feeling very sorry for myself. I was trying to cheer myself up by monitoring my progress: counting the steps that I had walked that day, listening to my breathing, congratulating myself on being able to do my shoelaces. Believe it or not, some of all that has got compressed down into that little poem. Well, actually, it's got compressed down into one phrase: 'cliff fall'. I fully understand that other people reading what I wrote might not 'get' that that's what I was on about. That's OK, because at the moment I wrote it, the only person 'getting' it was me. The writer is the first reader of what that writer writes! The point about this kind of writing is that you want it to do some 'work' for you. You want to see if you've expressed how you are or were. You want to see where your state of mind or health fits into the world of other people or nature. Are you a tree? A river? I was a weedy bloke staggering along on the sand while the world was young and massive and permanent around me. Then afterwards, when I heard the news, I was a fallen cliff. I was in the world. The world was in me.

Does that sound like a fun way to write? I hope so.
Now here's another:

> I'm a traveller who reached
> the Land of the Dead.
> I broke the rule that said I had to stay.
> I crossed back over the water,
> I dodged the guard dog,
> I came out.
> I've returned.
> I wander about.
> I left some things down there.
> It took bits of me prisoner:
> an ear and an eye.
> They're waiting for me to come back.
> The ear is listening.
> The eye is the lookout.

What have I done with this poem? I've taken a
story that already exists and put myself into it. Now let
me explain my thinking: I was (and still am) mystified
and troubled by my 40-day coma. It feels mysterious,
frightening, troubling, weird, comical, amazing. I've
seen pictures of myself in the coma: I look dead. I am
looking on myself as I think I might look when I die. If
you know *A Christmas Carol*, this is what Scrooge gets to
see, and it not only terrifies him but the sight of it
causes him to change his character.

In order to help ourselves deal with mysterious, troubling and frightening things, we can probe them to find out what they were really, really like. I've already described this with my investigations into meningitis. I do the same with Covid. Another way is to probe it by comparing it to other stories. You may or may not like or agree with Sigmund Freud, but one of the amazing things he does in his writing is compare what he has come to think by investigating the mind with what we see in stories like *Hamlet* or *Oedipus*. The moment we find similarities or analogies between our own lives and what we find in other stories, we become less alone. We are with other people who have also struggled with what we struggle with.

The story I've borrowed for that poem is *The Odyssey*. Odysseus manages to break the rule by getting to the land of the dead and getting out again. In a way, I felt that I had done that. It happens to a lot of us. I was staying in the French Pyrenees. My friends had their roots amongst the people in the village. One old man was very ill one night but he survived. In the morning, he was amazed to wake up. He told the father of my friends that he had thought during that night he had gone to the land of the moles ('la terre des taupes'). To understand and explain how he felt, he created (or borrowed) a little myth. That expression, 'the land of the moles', joins him to other people and to nature. It makes him less lonely. I've done the same with my 'traveller' story.

I've also added my own little myths in a similar tone as the original. I've slotted my particular condition (dodgy eye and ear) into the Greek myth. Actually, I've probably nicked it from other stories where there are lookouts – perhaps when Jim in *Treasure Island* has to be a lookout. So that's another thing we can do when we write: mix and blend stories, myths and legends, slotting ourselves into them as characters or lookers-on or passers-by.

Or, you can create a whole piece that is your own myth. Here's something I wrote:

> Gone
> we ran towards her
> but the van moved off
> we ran faster
> she reached out for us
> the van moved faster
> we reached for her hand
> she stretched out of the back of the van
> we ran, reaching
> the van got away
> we stopped running
> we never reached her
> before she was gone

From my point of view, it's not a 'true' story – I know it didn't happen in real life. There was no van. There was no 'us' trying to reach the van. I wrote this so that I could do some 'work' to understand something that had happened and perhaps so that I could get to feel better. This is how it panned out. You'll know from an earlier chapter that my mother died. It was an awful time, and we thought she was going to get better. I think she thought she was going to get better too. Afterwards, I had the sense – as do many people in my shoes – that she was 'taken away'. There is a very literal way in which dead people get 'taken away' – in ambulances and hearses. I mused on that. I daydreamed and it turned into what you've just read.

I thought, *I don't need ambulances and hearses.* The bit that I wanted to focus on is that idea of us wanting to hang on to her, and her not wanting to go. We're each, on both sides, stretching out to each other. That is a metaphorical idea, but I wanted to express this feeling of trying to hang on to her through a picture from the real world. So, I've got the idea of a van moving off. The van image is doing 'symbolic' work. It is what it is – a picture taken from real life, it's not fairies or nymphs – which I have made 'represent' what I felt like.

When you explore an event from real life, one you think symbolises a feeling you have, the real-life event 'holds you' or lifts you up like it's a life jacket. Again, you don't have to fill the scene up with 'feeling words'. You can let the scene do the work. The scene will affect you, the writer-reader. You will feel sympathy for 'her' stretching out of the back of the van, and again for the people stretching to reach her. None of those people are you, but your feelings are with them.

We say that our feelings are 'subjective' – a word often used to mean personal or private. Other things that are 'out there', not affected by us, are sometimes called 'objective' – like science, or when someone tries to describe something fairly and truthfully. A poem like this is quite strange: I've poured the 'sub-jective' (my feelings) into the 'objective' (a scene taken from real life). All my personal feelings are funnelled into the truth of an us, her and a van – a seemingly real-life scene.

We could call this 'objectivising experience'. So instead of something being purely or only ours, snarled up in our mind, it has become something 'out there'. In fact, once I've written it, I can compare the seemingly real scene I've created with my personal feelings. Have I got it right? Is it how I felt? Is it how I feel now?

This kind of writing and thinking can take the edge off pain. It can take us away from that desperate, nowhere-to-go, living-in-hell feeling and transport us for a while into something much calmer, cooler, more detached. It may or may not last. It may be one step amongst many more steps.

Sometimes people don't know how to begin, or worry about their writing not being 'good enough', but in truth we can write down a list of any kinds of words to make a story. This reminds us that we don't have to express ourselves through sentences. Sometimes sentences do a very good job. As you can see, I'm trying as hard as I can in this book to express things through sentences. And sometimes it is very hard. I'm right at the very edge of what I understand and what I hope you'll find useful. The great advantage of sentences is that they have a logic all of their own, that we often already know, even if it's subconsciously, because of our own experiences communicating.

In English, sentences often have a bit at the beginning which is usually the thing or idea or topic of the sentence (the 'subject'). Then you have what this beginning part does or feels or announces (the 'verb'). Then you might have something that is affected by this, or influenced by it, or has something done to it (the 'object') . You may also have add-ons that tell us about when, where, how this is going on, or the conditions under which they might happen, or an acceptance that this is happening in spite of something else or because of something else or in connection to something else (these are coordinate and subordinate clauses). In summary: 'subject'; 'verb'; 'object' + 'subordinate' or 'coordinate' clause of time, place, condition, concession and so on.

These are structures which we use all day, every day. We go about saying things like 'The bus is late' or 'I missed the bus because I wanted to watch the rest of the programme'. It's no big deal, and we don't need to know what each part is called in order to be able to use them. We just come up with these thoughts and they fit into the places waiting for them! It's a bit like fitting pieces into a jigsaw.

Some people call these places 'rules'. I don't. What's more, writers – and you can be a writer anytime anywhere – are constantly playing with these places, changing the rules to find our own means of expression. All of this means that your sentences don't need to be logical, or to stick to the rules.

You might feel that you have a torrent of feelings in your head. Or maybe it's other people saying or doing things and you've caught a stream of it, without fully making sense of the whole. Or maybe it's something tangled or knotty and you just want to hang on to what feels like the important stuff. Or there's a sequence but you're not quite sure what it is and you can't quite remember it until you write it down, like a shopping list . . .

. . . all these are situations which call for another way of writing, I think. One way of trying to do this has a name: 'stream of consciousness'. It's a phrase that suggests you know what's going on but it's all in a flow. Some famous writers have written like this: Virginia Woolf and James Joyce are two of them. I'm not saying that to put you off – far from it – it's just that you might want to take a look at them writing like that. Better still, give it a go yourself. Pick any moment from your life, when the things going on around you or the things going on in your mind feel like a stream or a rush or that they flow without a break. Dreams can be like that, so you could try it with a dream too.

Here's one of mine:

> I'm down
> I'm down the Underground
> Waiting
> Waiting for a train
> There's the platform
> There's the lines
> There's the tunnel
> There's the lines.
> I'll wait down there
> Down between the lines
> Waiting for the train
> Down between the lines
> I'll climb down there
> Down between the lines

and wait for the train
down there.
Look
Look up the tunnel look
Yes it's coming, it's coming
they say,
And it is.
And I'm between the lines.
And I can see it
See it coming
and I'm between the lines.
Can someone give me a
hand up?
Can't you see?
I'm between the lines
and the train's coming.
Can't you see?
I'm between the lines
and the train's coming.
Give me a hand someone
give me a hand
the train's coming
give me a hand
I can't climb up.
The train's coming
and the platform's sliding in
toward me too
with the train still coming

coming down the tunnel
the platform's sliding
sliding in towards me too.
I'm still down
Can't anyone see me
down between the lines?
Look
see
me
the train
platform
me
the train
near now
nearer now
nearer and nearer now
NOW
That's all.

This was an attempt to write about a nightmare I used to have when I was a child. I used to dread having it because I found it so frightening. You can write about dreams in many different ways, but I chose this way because I wanted to feel 'in' the dream and if anyone was going to read it, I wanted them to feel as if they were 'in' it too.

As you can see, I have written it with a mixture of sentences (as I described earlier) and some words or phrases that are not sentences. I felt as I wrote that writing whole sentences all the time held me up, or slowed me down. I also wanted to get hold of the idea of things happening again and again or constantly. You can state that, of course – 'this happened again and again'. Or you can show it by repeating the words that express the thing going on and on. Repetition is a great way to express things that carry on, especially if they're things that bother you or worry you.

If you're writing just for yourself, in order to help yourself, sometimes concentrating on the words that express this sense of being 'in' something carrying on and on is a great help. It's as if you've grabbed it and got it in your grasp – well, at least for as long as you're writing it. This can be a relief.

You may also find something else a bit satisfying: when you repeat words and phrases, and when you 'unfold' them on to a page, under each other, you start to make rhythms. A lot of word-rhythms in poems and songs come with rhymes, as with rap, for example. That's great and I'd recommend spending time doing that, but straight repetition without rhyme is easier and quicker to do. You get the result straightaway.

English is a language where we put 'stress' on some parts of words more than others. If I ask you to say, 'diddle, diddle, dumpling', the chances are you'll put more 'stress' on the 'didd' and 'dump' parts of those words than you will on the 'le' and 'ling' parts.

So that's like a drummer who hits a beat hard first, then soft.

Thinking back to the word games at the beginning of this chapter, you can doodle about by exploring these 'stressed' and 'unstressed' parts of words. You can do it just by playing with your name. My name has the rhythm TUM-te TUM-te. 'Michael Rosen' is the same rhythm as 'Humpty Dumpty'! In my nightmare poem there are some lines where I've tried to keep a rhythm going. At other times, I've changed it, or created a break.

So this brings together a) 'playing with the sound of words' with b) 'trying to create meaning and feeling'. I've now made something that is quite easy to write sound complicated! If you experiment yourself, though, you may well find it an absorbing, relaxing and satisfying thing to do.

Finally, let me show you something else.

Some situations and feelings feel so difficult that they seem impossible. Might there be a way of expressing this – perhaps understanding it – that conveys this impossibility back to us? Might there be a way of saying this without saying directly, over and over again, 'this feels impossible'? I sometimes think that saying something like 'this feels impossible' doesn't help me. It keeps me stuck in the impossibility! What if, then, I try to express the impossible thing using 'impossible language'?

Once, I was working with some children looking at some photos taken in what was known as a Jewish Ghetto during the Second World War. One of the photos was of a couple looking idyllically happy, as they stared up at a tree. Meanwhile, there were other photos showing desperate people, starving and dying. There were people lying in the middle of the pavements.

We talked about how desperate people must have felt, and yet there were some with hope. I wondered out loud about the idea of 'impossible language'. We talked about the idea that maybe instead of saying 'the man is lying on the pavement', we could say, 'the pavement spreads out underneath the man' or 'the tree takes the eyes of the couple'.

Later, I wrote:

> Today
> The rain has died
> My shoes have died
> The sun has died
> My coat has died
> The earth has died
> Today.
> One day
> The rain will flower
> My shoes will laugh
> The sun will sing

> My coat will fly
> The earth will dance
> One day.

Each of these lines are pictures (or images) of impossible things: one half terrible and hopeless, the other half full of joy and hope. I've also done what writers of poems, songs, movies, plays and stories have done for thousands of years: make the world around the 'teller' of the poem feel like the teller (whoever that might be). So here there are not only shoes and a coat, there is also the sun, the rain and the earth. This puts the person who owns the shoes and coat into the world of rain, sun and earth. The rain, sun and earth 'feel' what that person feels.

I've also tried to express the sense of having two different thoughts at the same time, one as strong as the other, one full of despair, the other full of hope. Perhaps they cancel each other out. Perhaps, as the hopeful one comes second, there is more on the hope side than on the despair. What do you think?

You might want to have a go at writing like this: trying out 'impossible writing' to express difficult moments and feelings. Perhaps, if you do, at least in that moment of writing, if not for longer, the impossible will feel possible.

I could go on showing how we can write as a way to get better, but all these ways that I've talked about follow the same path. I'm saying, 'Here is a bit of writing – you could write like that, if you wanted to.' Let's call that a method. The method is: you read something, you say to yourself I could write like that, then you have a go. You can use this method for any bit of writing that you read or hear. Let's call it the 'Like That Method'. Some people call it the 'imitate and invent' method. You start by imitating what you've read but you'll end up inventing something new – sometimes a little bit new, sometimes a lot.

Whichever it is and however you write, it's up to you.

Remember, the blank page is your friend: it doesn't laugh at you, it doesn't sneer at you. It doesn't say that you're no good. It doesn't say, 'Who do you think you are, kidding yourself you can write?' It just takes what you write. It's just there for you. And when you write on the blank page, what you've written is there for you to look at and think about. If you want to, you can then share it.

That's a bit different from sharing something just by talking to a person. If you write something and share it, you're sharing something you've unfolded on to a page, making it into a shape. It's you, but in a way it's not you, because now it's out there, separate from you.

Chapter 11

Raisins to be cheerful

I love raisins. They make me happy. I tell children that my secret name is Michael Raisin.

In this final section, I thought that I would collect together the short thoughts and tips that I tell myself when times are tough. Some of them I've mentioned through the book, others are here now for the first time, and I hope some of them might be useful to you!

FIRST – THE PHYSICAL STUFF

The point here is that if you don't sort out the physical stuff, you can't sort out the mental stuff. And anyway, as you take control of the physical stuff, it helps with the mental stuff. I tell myself over and over again that my mind is part of my body and my body is in my mind. What does 'my body is in my mind' mean? Everything we do with our bodies is controlled by our minds and we hold pictures and visions of what our body looks like and can do. Even when the weather or lovers or accidents or bullets do things to our bodies, our bodies react through what our minds ask them to do.

Breathing: If we lead fairly inactive lives (as I do), then our breathing is shallow. If our breathing is shallow, we are not exercising a good few parts of our body. Try this: breathe in through your nose to the count of four. Hold for one or two. Breathe out as slowly as you can through pursed lips. I check that I don't raise my shoulders or scrunch up my neck when I breathe in. I feel my chest widen sideways. I try to do this as often as I can. It can be both a way to relax and to clear my mind. The more I concentrate on my breathing, the less I feel twitchy and nervy.

Eating: I say to myself: I must eat as much fresh food as I can – salad, veg and fruit; drink six glasses of water a day. Avoid salt, sugar and alcohol, Michael.

I seek out favourite foods with the flavours or textures I like – I mean other than chocolate, cake, chips and cheese! I call it developing a good sense of hummus (because one of the foods is hummus).

Digestion: I work on the principle that I should never be constipated. The less you drink, the more water the body extracts from your bowel to compensate. Result: blockage! I also eat loads of food that has fibre in it, or 'roughage', like wholemeal bread or crackers like Ryvita, a lot of fruit, dried fruit and veg of all kinds. Prunes and dried figs are worth eating every day. I do. And raisins. Of course. Brits tend to get embarrassed talking about this stuff. I'm not – which you now know.

Walking: My aim is five 30-minute walks a week. I don't always manage it. As I walk, I try to do the breathing thing. I check how I walk. I try to walk evenly and lightly. I try not to jar my stride. I try to walk fast enough to be at least a bit out of breath. Walking is a great way to think. I find that after about 15 minutes, I start to get helpful thoughts.

Stretching: I see if I can stretch as many of my muscles as I can. We hold tension, irritation and trauma in our muscles. That's because we contract them every time we feel worried, sad, bad or in real trouble. Gently stretching the big muscles in our legs and back is a way of releasing some of this held-in anxiety and pain. I don't do it violently or in a hurried way. I try to imitate a cat – slow, long stretches.

The best stretch for back ache is to lie on a carpet

or rug on the floor and bring your knees up to your chest, holding them with your hands behind your knees. This gently stretches the long muscles of your back. The muscles in the backs of my legs (the hamstrings) need a lot of stretching. Easiest way is to put my hand on a post or table at about waist level and put one leg forwards. Then I pull my toes back towards my head, while I bend a small amount downwards, as if I'm going to tie up my shoelaces but never get there. I feel the hamstrings pull. It feels like a twinge that might be almost a bit uncomfortable. A bit painful in a nice kind of way.

Pains: We all get pains in our bodies some of the time. If there is no medical cause (like arthritis – which I've got!), the pains are often because of the way we become uneven or lopsided in the way we sit, get up, walk and the like. If I get a muscular pain somewhere, I've found it may get much better from a lot of gentle stretching. Or I play a game: experiment with repositioning my body as I walk or sit. I've found that I hold one shoulder much higher than another. And I twist to one side. I see if I can compensate for it. It's really, really hard but I've found that it works.

The core: About ten (or was it 20?) years ago, the body specialists started talking to us about the 'core'. These are the muscles at the front of our bodies that enable us to support ourselves in an upright position, whether we're walking or sitting. If our core is weak, our backs take the strain. There are all sorts of core exercises we can do, some brutal, some quite enjoyable, some quite likely to do an unfit person damage!

One way to strengthen your core is to build the strengthening into your everyday movement or 'use'. If you're sitting, you can keep reminding yourself to lengthen upwards, straightening your spine while dropping your shoulders. If you're standing, you can try doing the 'brace': lengthen upwards, drop your shoulders, hold your arms flexed down in front of you and imagine they're pulling away from you and you're pulling your body away from them. Or, try dropping your shoulders while lifting your arms away from your body, but keeping them floppy. See if you can feel your core as you do this.

Keep thinking all the time that you're lengthening your body. Not in any fierce way but as part of a gentle push upwards. Check your neck. Don't scrunch it up. As you stretch upwards, try to make the muscles up the sides of your neck do the work.

You can do these simple movements anytime anywhere. They are different from 'doing exercises'. They are about how you use your body all the time.

Look at how other people move, sit and stand.

Compare how some people use their muscles to support their skeletons and others seem to be pulling against their skeleton, twisting it down or hunching it or scrunching it. I think of myself in a constant but gentle struggle with all this. There's no winning, there's just the doing.

Sleep: We need sleep. We need it to rest our minds and bodies. If you have any bother about getting to sleep or staying asleep, it's a great idea to come up with a routine to help you. The best I've found is the breathing exercise I've mentioned, along with a muscle game. As I breathe, I concentrate on a group of muscles that I can feel responding to my breathing. It might be my ribs, or the bottom of my back. (Sometimes I try to flatten my back as I breathe, imagining that I'm breathing in through the base of my back.) Whichever part of my body I concentrate on, I try to really stick with it as I'm counting through my breathing. I make sure I'm not scrunching or hunching my neck or shoulders.

This works for me.

As I have an enlarged prostate – too much information? – some nights I have to get up to do a pee. I make sure to do pelvic floor moves to really empty my bladder – much too much information? – and after all that it could be quite easy to not fall back to sleep. I find the breathing trick, along with the muscle-focus game, does the trick.

AND NOW THE MIND

Most of this book has been about me thinking, talking and writing my way out of difficulty, loss, pain and illness.

Here are some themes I've picked out to say a bit more about.

Play: I guess you've picked up that I quite often cope by coming up with jokey names for things. Other times, I try to cope through experimenting – trying things out, playing games. These are all ways of playing. The opposites of play are things like taking orders and following routines without knowing why. Play is about you doing things because they amuse you. I think of play as 'trial and error without fear of failure'. I find that whatever I can do with that spirit in mind is a help, because it's me doing the playing. I'm in charge. I'm making up my own rules. We can change the rules, whether it's how we make a cake, grow flowers, sing in the bath or kick a ball about with our children.

Curiosity: I know in myself there are times when I shut down and stop asking questions. That's when I'm afraid or I feel small or ignorant or unwanted. They are depressing places to be. Curiosity is about wanting to know more, about anything: weather, how houses are built, our grandmother's life, birds, trains – anything. We can build into curiosity the idea of challenge, as well. I say to myself that I 'know' something, but then I challenge what I know with the possibility that there is something else out there that will change what I know. Some people come out of school not feeling very curious about anything. It's almost as if we have to try to learn how to be as curious as a two-year-old all over again. Curiosity didn't kill the cat. Curiosity is life.

Daydreaming: My daydreaming seems to go in two directions – backwards and forwards. Backwards daydreaming is thinking about all of the weird, painful, odd, hilarious, absurd, and tragic things that have happened to me. I call it archaeology of the mind, digging up stuff that has gone on 'back then' and wondering about it. Forwards daydreaming is about fantasies of what I could be, could have, thinking about things I yearn for.

In the backwards daydreaming, I can try to remake past events. So long as I remind myself that what's done is done and I can't do anything about it, it's no bad thing to play. Too much regret, though, can bring me down. Forwards daydreaming is really imagination: a place where I can go where 'my' world doesn't have to be the way it is, but also where I can imagine 'the' world doesn't have to be the way it is.

If we want to, we can make daydreaming a great motivator for us. It's as if daydreaming is a great pool of stuff – when we drink it in, it gives us energy to get up and go. For me, daydreaming is what makes it possible for me to write, which leads straight into . . .

Creativity: Creativity is making new things, changing things in new and different ways. It's at the heart of all the inventions and creations of the human race: art, discovery, technology, architecture, farming and our cultures – in how we cook, do our hair, clothe ourselves, worship, talk and write. Creativity is us. It makes us what we are, it made us what we were and it'll make our future: how to deal with climate change, disease and poverty.

That's the big stuff. But creativity is within each of us. It's part of us to be creative with the things around us and in our relationships with others and with the institutions and organisations we make. The things around us are materials – flour, water, wood, even our own bodies. There can be creativity in our relationships – how we love or how we bring up children. The institutions we make – our schools, hospitals and workplaces – are also things to be creative with, which leads into how we organise our society, and how we make and distribute the things we need for the good of those in it.

Creativity can be what I doodle on the back of an envelope as I wait for a train, how I decide to put a new herb into my salad dressing, how I design a house (not me! Though I did once solve a builder's problem with a staircase and a landing!), and on all the way to imagining how we're going to get out of the many messes the human race gets into.

Whichever of these we get involved with, being creative feels like we're renewing and revitalising ourselves alongside and with the people around us. In every single thing we do, we can be encouraged to be more creative, or discouraged. I have a choice. The one will make me feel good, the other one will slowly weigh me down. It's the difference between always thinking of the possible and going along with what's there just because it's there.

Thinking of the possible and trying out new things makes me feel better.

Cooperation: Just above, I mentioned how creativity works 'alongside and with the people around us'. This is hard work, but actually we don't have a choice. Everything about human life involves coexistence and cooperation. We can feel alone or even pretend we are a lone, self-sufficient person, but if we work or shop or talk, we become part of a complex world of people cooperating to make and sell things and even to create language itself. Even when we're alone with nature (as we believe), this 'nature' everywhere on the planet is affected by what humans have done – the weather, the sea, the land. At the heart of it all are various kinds of cooperation. Even war is cooperation! Armies are huge organisations of people cooperating and there's even a ghastly way in which warring sides cooperate in the 'game' of war.

Of course, the kinds of cooperation I'm talking about are to do with partners, families, projects, campaigns, local plans and workplaces. These are where we can be equal partners in planning something we care about and want to happen: a holiday, a school fete, a campaign to save a local building, improving accessibility for disabled people, a trade-union decision or any other kind of social matter.

What's fantastic and uplifting is when cooperation really works and everyone's voice is heard and respected, where decisions are made that people are happy with, and where the outcome is good. I don't pretend for a moment that this is easy. What I do think, though, is that it's necessary. Without it, we end up in distress, conflict and trauma.

One thing to be proud of: I'll just repeat my 'One Good Thing Principle' from earlier in the book one more time. Every day, I try to do at least one thing which, as I shut my eyes to go to sleep, I can focus on and say to myself, 'I did OK. I'm pleased I did that.'

Commitment: It's very easy to not care about much. There's something strange about the apparatuses we've built around ourselves. If we can afford enough 'stuff' – shopping, TV, computers, phones, whatever – then we can think it's all taken care of. I guess for some that's OK, until something big comes along and knocks us over. Another way of looking at being alive is to think that there's not much point in doing it (being alive, that is!) unless we're committed to something bigger than ourselves, something that involves other people.

I guess I don't need to say this, but another crucial part of surviving and getting or feeling better is finding at least one person who wants to be committed to you. That's not very easy, is it? If you have a partner and your parents are still alive and you have children, that's hopefully more than one person. If you have wider family or great friends or committed colleagues or people who love what you do for them, or with them, it'll be even more people. The circle gets wider and wider.

I've met people who are committed to even more people than that. For a few months in 2020, these were people who were committed to saving my life, keeping me alive, and then helping me to stand up and teaching me how to move and walk. They were doing just the same for hundreds of others at the same time. I sometimes say, I tried to die but they wouldn't let me. Perhaps it's better to say that the lives of thousands and thousands of us are in danger every day, and these wonderful people don't let us die. They help us get better.